LAW FOR DOCTORS

HOW MEDICAL PROFESSIONALS CAN
PROTECT THEIR LICENSE, ASSETS,
INCOME, AND LEGACY

Zachariah B. Parry, Esq.

1.21 GIGAWATTS
PUBLISHING

Copyright © 2023 The Fortune Law Firm

F | FORTUNE
LAW FIRM

All rights reserved. No part of this publication may be reproduced, distributed, or transmitted in any form or by any means, including photocopying, recording, or other electronic or mechanical methods, without prior written permission of the publisher, except in the case of brief quotations embodied in critical reviews and certain other noncommercial uses permitted by copyright law.

Distributed nationally by 1.21 Gigawatts Publishing.

Las Vegas | Highland | Minneapolis | Baton Rouge

Hardcover ISBN: 979-8-86717-114-8
Paperback ISBN: 979-8-86716-793-6

Cover design by Zachariah B. Parry through the MidJourney app on a private Discord server.

Manufactured and printed in the United States of America.

DEDICATION

To the physicians, doctors, dentists, surgeons, chiropractors, psychiatrists, nurses, physician's assistants, nurse practitioners, pharmacists, and all other medical practitioners who take risks every day to make our lives better but who do not get enough recognition or thanks. This book is for you.

DISCLAIMER

Hey! Zach Parry here.

I hate to have to start my book off with a disclaimer, but I am a lawyer, after all. The information I have compiled in this book is meant to provide you with some very valuable information related to legal protections. Protections from the National Practitioner Data Bank. Protections against potential creditors. Your patients. Your employees. Protections against probate. Taxes.

I have made painstaking efforts to ensure everything in this book is well researched and accurate, but I can't guarantee that I didn't rely on misleading information or that things haven't changed between when I wrote it and when you read it. The legal world is very complicated and constantly changing and legislation, regulations, administrative decisions, and common law all vary state to state.

Additionally, there are never any guarantees in the law. It could be indisputable that you were speeding, but one officer gives you a ticket and another does not. Similarly, different judges apply the same laws differently. Protections you set up may be ineffective: you could do everything right and still lose.

The information in this book is not intended to convey legal or financial advice specific to you or your circumstances. So before you rush off and change what you're doing based on something you've read in my book, please consult with a lawyer (but be careful whom you choose—there are a lot of charlatans out there), and make sure you are getting individualized advice based on your particular circumstances and goals.

If you have questions, you can reach me here:

zach@thefortunelawfirm.com.

TABLE OF CONTENTS

Dedication iii

Disclaimer v

Introduction xiii

Part I: Protecting Your License 1

    Chapter 1: The National Practitioner Data Bank: A Road Paved with Good Intentions 3

        The Government's Fix 7

        The National Practitioner Data Bank 9

        The NPDB – A Sex Offender Registry for Doctors 9

        Medical Professionals v. Criminals – A Comparison 11

    Chapter 2: Has the NPDB Had Its Intended Effect? 15

        Getting Blacklisted – What Does It Mean? 17

    Chapter 3: Keeping Your Name off the Data Bank: Prophylactic and Reactionary Measures 23

        Hanged by an Inferred Comma 24

        Who Has to Report Payments? 26

        What Constitutes a Malpractice Action or Claim? 28

        What About the Report Itself? 33

Chapter 4: How Do These Exceptions Benefit the Practitioner? 39
    You've Got Patient Contracts: Use Them! 39
    The Patient Doesn't Have to Follow the Contract for You to Be Protected 43
    If Only Individual Practitioners Get Reported, Not Groups, then Become a Group! 44
    Let's Talk Practicality: How Does It Work? 45
    Attempts to Eliminate the Corporate Shield 48

Chapter 5: Protecting Yourself from Your Patients (While Protecting Them, Too!) 53
    Why Patients Sue Doctors 54
    Don't Avoid the Patient When Something Goes Wrong; Consider Apologizing 57
    Practice Medicine, Not Defensive Medicine 60
    Use a Checklist 62
    How to Properly Terminate a Patient 63

Chapter 6: Protect Yourself from Your Employees (and from the Actions of Your Employees) 71
    Proper Hiring 72
    Proper Training 73

Part II: Protecting Your Assets 83
  Chapter 7: Introduction to Liability 85
    Sidebar: Where Does Insurance Fit into This? 88
  Chapter 8: Built-in Statutory Protections 93
    Homestead Protection 94
    Social Security Payments and Other Government Benefits 95
    Private Retirement Accounts 95

Permanent Life Insurance 96

Chapter 9: Protecting Yourself with a Business Entity 99

    A Brief History of the Corporation and Limited Liability Company 99

    Corporation v. Limited Liability Company – Which One Is Better? 102

    The Tax Election 103

    How Business Entities Protect Your Assets 104

Chapter 10: Maintaining Your LLC 111

    Alter Ego: A Question of Separateness 112

Chapter 11: Business Ownership Best Practices 119

    Personal Use of Company Assets and Vice Versa 123

    Two Businesses Sharing Office Space, Employees, or Both 124

Chapter 12: The Series LLC 129

    How Are Series LLCs Taxed? 131

    What If I Live in a State That Doesn't Have Its Own Version of a Series LLC? 132

    Potential Downside of the Series LLC 136

    I Have a Series LLC 137

Chapter 13: The Asset Protection Trust 141

    Spendthrift Provisions 142

    Self-Settled Trusts 145

    Full Faith and Credit v. Conflict of Laws 147

Part III: Protecting Your Income (Reducing Your Taxes) 151

Chapter 14: Paying the Minimum Self-Employment Taxes 152

    What if Your Business Does Not Make Enough to Pay Your Reasonable Salary? 157

What if Your Business Is Really Successful and You Have Enough to Pay Far More Distributions Than Salary? 157

How Does This Knowledge Save You in Taxes? 157

When You Might Want to Pay More in Salary than You Have To 158

Chapter 15: Tax Strategies for Business Owners 159

How Taxes Work 160

The Augusta Rule 162

The Home Office Deduction 164

Hire Your Children 166

How Else Can You Save? 167

Part IV: Protecting Your Legacy 171

Chapter 16: The Revocable Living Trust 173

Example: The Special Needs Trust 175

The Revocable Living Trust 176

Chapter 17: The Revocable Living Trust – Speaking for You When You Cannot 179

General Power of Attorney 180

Healthcare Power of Attorney 183

Life-Prolonging Measures 184

Organ Donation 185

Guardianship Provisions – For the Testators 186

Guardianship Provisions – For Minor Children 189

Final Wishes or Funeral Instructions Document 190

Chapter 18: The Revocable Living Trust – A Seamless Transition of Property to Your Heirs 192

Conclusion 197

Further Information 199

About the Author 201

Acknowledgments 203

INTRODUCTION

I spent the first decade-plus of my professional career in the courtroom. At the beginning of my journey, I was less discerning about what kind of case I would take—property law, probate, family law, breach of contract, construction defect, employment law, fraud, and even some criminal defense.

I helped a mother defeat a request for a restraining order brought by her daughter, who wanted to showcase mom's "abuse" so she could go live with dad, who was a much more permissive parent.[1]

I found myself litigating a boundary dispute over the matter of a tiny sliver of property between the backyards of two middle-class families in Boulder City, Nevada.

I represented a father who had been paying child support for sixteen years for a child who wasn't his.

I represented a stone and tile subcontractor in a case where a wealthy homeowner claimed the tiles in her foyer were not perfectly level.

At one point, I was involved in a defamation case against Wayne Newton.

I was a trial lawyer, though I did mostly injury cases. I started on the defense side, representing the hotels, casinos, grocery store chains, and other typically large corporations.

Then I started my own firm and represented the injured parties. I went after those big businesses. And medical professionals.

---

[1] I recall that case fondly: my "co-counsel" and I were law students at the time, and opposing counsel was a professor at my law school. It was as much fun beating the professor as it was helping the mother.

To me, you were all in the same category. People making lots of money, careless in your professions, and heedless of who you hurt along the way.

I learned there were no absolutes in the law. The opposing party wasn't always a bad guy. In fact, more often than I wanted, my own client was the one in the wrong (a fact, which, once discovered, meant I would no longer represent them).

As I took more and more cases against medical professionals, I realized just how hard you had it.

You warn your patient of the risks, but the bad outcome is still your fault.

Your patient doesn't follow your directions, but the bad outcome is still your fault.

Your patient never pays you for the work you do, but they still want you to pay them.

You never even saw the patient, but they're in pain, and it's *your* fault!

It gets worse if there is litigation. If you don't settle the case, you risk losing everything at trial. If you do settle it, your name gets put on the blacklist for doctors.

What's more, being a doctor makes you a target beyond your professional life. Your daughter rear-ends someone? A guest of one of your tenants just injured themselves in one of your investment properties? The moment they find out you're a medical professional, the perceived value of the case skyrockets, and you find yourself fighting even harder to hold on to what's yours.

And although as a medical student you thought you'd have lots of money as soon as you started working, you realize that between student loans and taxes, you've got three mortgages, not just one. So instead of waiting just a few years to finally live that upscale lifestyle you worked so hard for, you find yourself in year ten, fifteen, or twenty before you can finally afford to relax a little bit. Except even then you can't because you've trained yourself not to take a moment to yourself.

Amidst all this it is easy to forget that you're a healer, and you got into this profession with a desire to, one patient at a time, make the world a little more bearable.

I hope the picture I painted doesn't resemble your life at all, but I suspect more of it resonated with you than you'd like.

So let's see what we can do to make your life a little easier.

I sold my trial practice several years ago and have dedicated myself since to protecting medical professionals.² I use what I call the four pillars of protection:

1. Protecting Your License
2. Protecting Your Assets
3. Protecting Your Income (Reducing Your Taxes)
4. Protecting Your Legacy

In the coming pages, let me show you some of the things I have learned in my profession that could help you in yours.

Also, I recommend you read the footnotes (or at least glance at them before you turn the page). I have worked hard not to make any assertions that aren't backed up by verifiable facts, and if you want to independently verify anything I've said, you should easily be able to do so. There's also a lot of fun to be had among the citations, so lighten the legal discussion by reading them!³

---

² Throughout the book, I use the following terms interchangeably: medical professionals, health care professionals, physicians, and doctors. Whichever term I use, I'm referring to medical practitioners in all fields. Although examples might involve a field of expertise that isn't yours, the general principles still apply.

³ You'll learn to distinguish quickly which are the footnotes that are references to legal sources and which ones are meant to make you smile.

PART I

Protecting Your License

CHAPTER 1

The National Practitioner Data Bank: A Road Paved with Good Intentions

Although the National Practitioner Data Bank was established in 1986, its story arguably starts in 1970s Astoria, Oregon[1] with an old boys' club of doctors called the Astoria Clinic.[2]

In 1972, the Astoria Clinic hired a general and vascular surgeon by the name of Timothy Patrick. Dr. Patrick must have impressed, because, within only a year, the partners at the clinic offered him a partnership position. Dr. Patrick declined the invitation and opened a competing independent practice instead. Astoria Clinic continued to employ Dr. Patrick while he worked concurrently at his independent practice. However, based on the actions that followed, they apparently interpreted his turning down their offer as a slight and were less than enthusiastic about having one of their own employees compete with them.

Both Dr. Patrick and the Astoria Clinic partners also served on the medical staff of Astoria's only hospital, Columbia Medical Hospital. (It was a very small town.)

For the next several years, the Astoria Clinic acted with hostility towards Dr. Patrick. Its doctors often refused to assist Dr. Patrick with his patients; they would not send him referrals, opting instead to send

---

[1] Astoria is a small coastal town in northwestern Oregon famous for being the hometown of the Goonies. It is also where *Short Circuit* (1986) and *Kindergarten Cop* (1990) were filmed within a few years of *Goonies* (1985).
[2] *Patrick v. Burget*, 486 U.S. 94, 96, 108 S. Ct. 1658, 1660, 100 L. Ed. 2d 83 (1988). All facts relating to Dr. Patrick described below are from this case.

patients to the next-closest surgeon, which was 50 miles away; and they would not enter cross-coverage agreements with him.

This tension escalated in 1979 when one of the Astoria Clinic partners submitted a complaint to Columbia Medical about Dr. Patrick. The complaint alleged that one of Dr. Patrick's newly hired associates had left a patient unattended.

Columbia Medical referred the complaint to the State Board of Medical Examiners (BME), where the case was assigned to a committee chaired by another of the partners of the Astoria Clinic. This partner authored a public reprimand of Dr. Patrick. When Dr. Patrick sought judicial review of the reprimand, the BME retracted the letter in its entirety.

In 1981, the Astoria Clinic attacked again, this time through one of its surgeons. The Clinic requested that Columbia Medical initiate a review of petitioner's hospital privileges, and in response, Columbia Medical (many of whose medical staff were partners at the Astoria Clinic—are you starting to see a theme here?) decided to terminate Dr. Patrick's privileges at what was still the only hospital in Astoria.

Dr. Patrick asked for an opportunity to be heard on the issue under the hospital's bylaws. The committee that oversaw the hearing was headed by the same Astoria Clinic partner who had initiated the complaint two years earlier, and when he and others from the Clinic refused to testify about their bias against him, Dr. Patrick voluntarily resigned from hospital staff rather than risk termination. He immediately filed a lawsuit.

In his lawsuit, Dr. Patrick alleged that the Astoria Clinic was using the peer-review process as a pretext for reducing the competition that the Astoria Clinic faced from him and his independent practice, violating antitrust law.

The case went to a jury trial, and the jury found that the Astoria Clinic had a "specific intent to injury or destroy competition." The court awarded Dr. Patrick $650,000 in antitrust damages, $2.2 million in treble damages, and $228,600 in attorney's fees.

Astoria Clinic appealed, and the Ninth Circuit, in 1986, reversed the decision. The court acknowledged that the Clinic acted in bad faith in bringing the complaints against Dr. Patrick but determined that participants in peer-review proceedings are immune from antitrust claims because the state of Oregon had given legislative approval of the peer-review process.

This case sent ripples through the press. But rather than emphasize the improper use of the peer-review process, the headlines focused on the incompetent physician who sued members of the peer-review committee investigating him and ended up winning millions.[3]

Dr. Patrick took his case to the United States Supreme Court and prevailed in getting this country's highest court to overturn the Ninth Circuit decision. And again, the press paraded the dangers of allowing peer-review panels to be sued,[4] and there was a general panic in the medical field as doctors were reluctant to serve on peer-review panels for fear of legal reprisal should a negative decision be made about the doctor being reviewed.

At about the same time Dr. Patrick's story was unfolding, the press was publishing another series of alarmist articles related to bad physicians doing harm in one state then jumping borders to another state, only to do harm again.[5] And again. And sometimes again and again.

In perhaps the most egregious case to be made public, Dr. Frederick Huffnagle was traipsing across the country doing medical harm: In 1970, in Connecticut, Dr Huffnagle performed an experimental hip surgery he had never done before, without doing a consultation first or having the proper equipment.[6] The operation was not what would be called a success. Beverly Hospital pulled his privileges as a result.

---

[3] *See* Kadar, N. "How Courts Are Protecting Unjustified Peer Review Actions Against Physicians by Hospitals," 16 *J. Am. Physicians & Surgeons* 17, 20 (2011). This is not unlike the infamous McDonald's hot coffee case. The headlines had people enraged, but anyone looking at the facts can see that the jury got it right and the headlines were misleading—McDonald's was clearly in the wrong. Thank you for being responsible, press!

[4] Savage, DG. May 17, 1988, *L.A. Times*, "Peer Review Teams That Censure Doctors Can Be Sued for Damages, Justices Hold," available at:
https://www.latimes.com/archives/la-xpm-1988-05-17-mn-2859-story.html, last accessed September 8, 2022.

[5] Van Tassel, KA. "Blacklisted: The Constitutionality of the Federal System for Publishing Reports of 'Bad' Doctors in the National Practitioner Data Bank," 33 *Cardozo L. Rev.* 2031, 2095 (2012) (citing Rosenberg, CL. "How Bad Doctors Dodge Discipline," 62 *Med. Econ.* 241 (1985) (reporting on 33 physicians who engaged in state hopping after negative state licensure proceedings); U.S. Gen. Accounting Office, GAO-84-53, "Expanded Federal Authority Needed To Protect Medicare and Medicaid Patients from Health Practitioners Who Lose Their Licenses," at iii, 7–8 (1984), available at http://www.gao.gov/assets/150/141458.pdf (identifying 39 doctors who relocated to new states after losing their license in another state and pointing out that far less than 1% of physicians have problems that lead to licensure sanctions, which translates into less than 1 per 1000 physicians).

[6] Van Tassel, *Blacklisted,* 33 *Cardozo L. Rev.* 2046 (citing "Small Percentage of Doctors Responsible for Surge in Malpractice Suits, Rates," *Bos. Globe,* June 15, 1986, at 1). All the following information on Dr. Huffnagle is taken from this law-review article.

Dr. Huffnagle headed across town to Hunt Memorial, where, after having no problem getting a job, he installed the wrong size artificial knee in a patient, which resulted in her permanent need of a wheelchair, a condition worse than the one she had before surgery. He continued to perform surgeries on other patients. Five medical malpractice suits and five payouts later, Dr. Huffnagle moved to California for a clean slate.

In California, Dr. Huffnagle lied to Westminster Hospital about his professional history and was able to obtain staff privileges. One year and four malpractice lawsuits later, he was terminated from Westminster. Dr. Huffnagle moved back east, this time to Massachusetts, where he started working for Massachusetts Osteopathic.[7]

The actions of Dr. Huffnagle and several other border-crossing bad-actor doctors took their toll. It only takes a small percentage of such doctors to drastically increase the cost of healthcare and malpractice insurance rates.

Indeed, several studies looked back on the period of the 1970s and 80s to try to identify and make sense of the maldistribution of malpractice claims.[8] One study analyzing a decade of claims from 2005–14 found that 1% of all physicians accounted for 32% of paid claims, and 94% of doctors were not responsible for any payments.[9]

As these cases were catching the public's attention in the mid-1980s, malpractice lawsuits were also at an all-time high,[10] "insurance companies were pulling out of markets and insurance costs were increasing at rates that were causing some physicians to leave the practice."[11]

---

[7] You gotta make a living, though, right?

[8] See, e.g., Taragin MI, Wilczek AP, Karns ME, Trout R, Carson JL. "Physician Demographics and the Risk of Medical Malpractice." 93 *Am J Med* 537–42 (1992); Sloan FA, Mergenhagen PM, Burfield WB, Bovbjerg RR, Hassan M. "Medical Malpractice Experience of Physicians: Predictable or Haphazard?" 262 *JAMA* 3291–97 (1989); Adamson TE, Baldwin DC Jr, Sheehan TJ, Oppenberg AA. "Characteristics of Surgeons with High and Low Malpractice Claims Rates." 166 *West J Med* 37–44 (1997); Ellis RP, Gallup CL, McGuire TG. "Should Medical Professional Liability Insurance Be Experience Rated? 57 *J Risk Insur* 66–78 (1990).

[9] Studdert DM et al., "Prevalence and Characteristics of Physicians Prone to Malpractice Claims," 374 *N. Engl. J. Med.* 354, 356 (2016).

[10] Vyas, D et√al. "Clinical Peer Review" 20 *WJG* 6357–63, available at https://www.researchgate.net/publication/262977889_Clinical_peer_review_in_the_United_States_History_legal_development_and_subsequent_abuse, last accessed September 9, 2022.

[11] Van Tassel, *Blacklisted*, 33 *Cardozo L. Rev.* 2042.

At the time, the most common way to address issues of physician competence was the peer-review panel—"the process by which physicians judge the competence of their fellow professionals and recommend disciplinary action for those found dangerously incompetent."[12] However, in the wake of the *Patrick* case, "physicians aggrieved by the results of peer review increasingly appeared in federal court claiming that the actions of their peers were anti-competitive and violated federal antitrust laws."[13]

These factors combined to create what many in the public considered a healthcare crisis, and this "crisis" pressured the government to intervene to fix it. This, like other governmental fixes, had both intended and unintended consequences.

The Government's Fix

We've reviewed the context of 1980s healthcare: reported incidence of malpractice was at an all-time high; doctors were free to scorch the earth in one state then move to another to start another campaign of harm; and the peer-review panel, one of the most oft-used ways to hold doctors to account, was falling out of favor because more and more doctors post-*Patrick* found themselves getting sued for imposing discipline, which discouraged others from being willing to participate.

Ron Wyden, a U.S. Legislator representing Oregon—the same state that produced the *Patrick* case—proposed legislation aimed at fixing the healthcare problem. The legislation, which was called the Health Care Quality Improvement Act of 1986 (HCQIA) made five findings that its drafters believed justified the introduction of this legislation:[14]

- The increasing occurrence of medical malpractice and the need to improve the quality of medical care have become nationwide problems that warrant greater efforts than those that can be undertaken by any individual state.
- There is a national need to restrict the ability of incompetent physicians to move from state to state without disclosure or

---

[12] *Manion v. Evans*, 986 F.2d 1036, 1037 (6th Cir. 1993).
[13] *Id.*
[14] Health Care Quality Improvement Act, Pub. L. No. 99–660, tit. IV, 100 Stat. 3784 (1986) (codified as 42 U.S.C. 11101 et al.). These bullet points are listed verbatim as they are in the statute.

discovery of the physician's previous damaging or incompetent performance.
- This nationwide problem can be remedied through effective professional peer review.
- The threat of private money damage liability under federal laws, including treble damage liability under federal antitrust law, unreasonably discourages physicians from participating in effective professional peer review.
- There is an overriding national need to provide incentive and protection for physicians engaging in effective professional peer review.

The HCQIA attempted to accomplish this in two parts. Part A of the statute created broad immunity for those on peer-review panels. It aimed to erase doctors' fear of liability associated with participating in the review and disciplinary process.[15] Part B implemented required reporting requirements for medical malpractice insurance companies making payments on behalf of their insured doctors, boards of medical examiners that impose discipline on physicians, and health care entities or professional societies that enforce certain limits on the doctor's privileges or membership.[16] To encourage proper reporting, strict monetary penalties were attached to an entity's failure to report.[17]

These reports were to be sent to the appropriate state licensing board and to "the Secretary [of Health and Human Services], or, in the Secretary's discretion, to an appropriate private or public agency which has made suitable arrangements with the Secretary with respect to receipt, storage, protection of confidentiality, and dissemination of the information under this part."[18]

That "appropriate private or public agency" that the Secretary designated was the United States Department of Health & Human Services. And the "receipt, storage ... and dissemination of the information" became the National Practitioner Data Bank.

---

[15] *Id.* at Part A.
[16] *Id.* at Part B.
[17] *Id.*
[18] *Id.* § 424(b).

The National Practitioner Data Bank

The National Practitioner Data Bank, or NPDB, was intended to prevent bad-actor doctors from being able to cross borders into states that were unaware, and had no easy way to become aware, of the practice history of those doctors seeking licensure to practice within their borders.

It would be hard to disagree with the intent. Stories of practitioners like Dr. Huffnagle are scary. Knowing they're real, and the person you are seeing for medical care could be another Dr. Huffnagle, makes it even more frightening.

The problem with the list is not the intent, but the execution. The NPDB reporting requirements cast far too wide of a net, are unappealable and permanent, and have created far-reaching, often severe consequences for the doctors who find their names on the list. Apart from being labeled a "blacklist," the NPDB has also been characterized as an "Orwellian nightmare," "Medical McCarthyism," "Big Brother," "Frankenstein," "scarlet letter," and akin to "Nazi Germany."[19]

The NPDB – A Sex Offender Registry for Doctors

The history of blacklists in the criminal justice system is a long and storied one that includes public shaming and permanent labeling to warn others of the criminal/sinner's past behavior.

Nathaniel Hawthorne famously explored the implications of one such British society in his classic work of fiction, *The Scarlet Letter*, but they also form a very real part of our American history:

> Burglary was punished in all the colonies by branding with a capital B in the right hand for the first offense, in the left hand for the second, "and if either be committed on the Lord's Daye his Brand shall beesett [sic] on his forehead as a mark of infamy." In Maryland, every county was ordered to have branding irons, with the lettering specifically prescribed: SL stood for seditious libel and could be burned on either cheek.

---

[19] Ryzen, E. "The National Practitioner Data Bank; Problems and Proposed Reforms,"13 *J. Legal Med.* 409, 444 (1992).

M stood for manslaughter, T for thief, R for rogue or vagabond, F for forgery.[20]

Branding as a socially acceptable way of warning others fell out of favor by the early 1800s, and through the next century and a half evolved into blacklisting, with the federal government adopting the practice for the first time in the McCarthy era of modern witch-hunts.[21]

The U.S. Supreme Court brought an end to the practice for communists in the 1960s,[22] and by the end of the 1980s, most criminal registries were disfavored and gone.[23]

However, after the publicity created by bad physicians like Dr. Huffnagle, lawmakers harnessed their fear into several legislative pen strokes, and like their colonist forebears who went too far in the name of protecting the public, the modern legislators sought to brand the bad actors to serve as a warning to everyone else. Instead of burning a mark into the skin, the NPDB would keep the bad doctors' names in a list. The brand, if not quite as visible, is just as permanent, and if not as physically painful, can have a huge psychological and financial impact.

Just a few years later, in the 1990s, perhaps emboldened by their previous success in creating a registry for bad doctors, state governments established another blacklist, this one for sex offenders. By 1995, every state had one, and in 2006, to create uniformity and broad application, the federal government adopted its own.[24]

It does not necessarily shock the conscience that to warn communities of a person's criminal proclivities we require the convicted's name and crime to be publicly registered. What might come as a surprise, though, is that the broad rights provided to sex offenders are not afforded to the same degree, and in many cases, not

---

[20] Van Tassel, *Blacklisted,* 33 *Cardozo L. Rev.* 2034–35, quoting Cox, JA. "Bilboes, Brands, and Branks: Colonial Crimes and Punishments," Spring *Colonial Williamsburg* (2003), available at
https://research.colonialwilliamsburg.org/Foundation/journal/spring03/branks.cfm, last accessed October 18, 2022.
[21] *Id.* at 2035–36.
[22] *Albertson v. Subversive Activities Control Bd.,* 382 U.S. 70, 86 S. Ct. 194, 15 L. Ed. 2d 165 (1965).
[23] Van Tassel, *Blacklisted,* 33 *Cardozo L. Rev.* at 2037.
[24] *Id.* at 2037–38. *See also* 42 U.S.C. § 16901 (2006).

at all, to medical professionals facing[25] their own permanent black mark.

Medical Professionals v. Criminals – A Comparison

The United States Constitution guarantees both substantive and procedural due process.[26] As part of those protections, someone who has been accused of a crime has the following rights, which constitute a "procedurally safeguarded opportunity to contest":

- An unbiased tribunal
- Notice of the proposed action and the grounds asserted for it
- Opportunity to present reasons why the proposed action should not be taken
- The right to present evidence, including the right to call witnesses
- The right to know opposing evidence
- The right to cross-examine adverse witnesses
- A decision based exclusively on the evidence presented
- Opportunity to be represented by counsel
- Requirement that the tribunal prepare a record of the evidence presented
- Requirement that the tribunal prepare written findings of fact and reasons for its decision[27]

This list of rights, which is well known and familiar to almost any criminally accused, will be unrecognizable to a physician who discovers their name is on the NPDB.[28]

To be fair, there are many ways for a physician's name to be reported (discussed below), and not all of them are devoid of due process. But even then, the process is not particularly fair.

For example, a physician who is sued certainly has due process rights in the litigation. They can collect evidence, cross-examine the

---

[25] To say that a medical professional "faces" their impending registry is not accurate, for that would require due process rights. In many cases, a physician's name is reported without the physician knowing about it at all.
[26] U.S. Const. Amends. 5 & 14.
[27] Friendly, HJ. "Some Kind of Hearing," 123 *U. Pa. L. Rev.* 1267, 1279–95 (1975).
[28] Unless that physician has also been through criminal proceedings. ☺

plaintiff patient at deposition or trial, present their own evidence in defense, etc. They have the same protections as any other litigant.

However, a settlement during litigation is almost always reportable, regardless of whether the physician has done anything wrong or made a mistake. These due process protections may ensure that the physician is treated fairly in litigation while doing nothing to protect a physician who has done everything right medically but settles for practical or nuisance purposes. Those "good" physicians are reported, too.

As the president of the Association of American Physicians and Surgeons put it in a letter to Congress, "damaging information is being entered into this data bank with no regard to accuracy. Good physicians are being reported to the Data Bank for reasons totally unrelated to patient care."[29]

In other words, even where due process applies to a physician in the truth-finding, it does nothing to protect the physician in the reporting, which often has little to do with the truths uncovered. Where the reporting is triggered by a settlement payment, the facts of the case have no bearing whatsoever.

Continuing our physician v. criminal comparison, few, if any, crimes have mandatory reporting. In fact, the idea of "pressing charges" gives victims some say in whether a criminal is prosecuted. Prosecutorial discretion allows the government to decline pursuing charges against known or suspected criminals. Only after someone has committed a crime, the government presses charges, and either the accused pleads guilty or proof "beyond a reasonable doubt" leads to a guilty verdict are criminals eligible to have their name registered. However, criminals are only subject to registration for certain egregious crimes, sexual crimes, or both.

The NPDB, on the other hand, has attendant mandatory reporting requirements. Malpractice insurance companies, state licensing boards, healthcare providers, the Department of Veterans Affairs, the Drug Enforcement Administration, and private professional societies like the American Medical Association and American Dental Association are all required to notify the NPDB of reportable events.[30]

---

[29] Jan 25, 2018, Letter from Albert L. Fisher, M.D "AAPS Tells Congress: NPDB is Flawed and Should Be Abolished," available at https://aapsonline.org/aaps-tells-congress-npdb-flawed, last accessed October 18, 2022.

[30] U.S. Gen. Accounting Office, GAO-01-130, "National Practitioner Data Bank: Major Improvements Are Needed to Enhance Data Bank's Reliability," at 7 (2000), available at https://www.gao.gov/assets/gao-01-130.pdf, last accessed October 18, 2022.

The standard of proof in these proceedings can vary from "completely subjective" to "preponderance of the evidence" (more likely true than not),[31] both of which fall far short of "beyond a reasonable doubt," which is the legal standard of proof in criminal cases.

Reportable events include the following:

- Medical malpractice payments
- Federal and state licensure and certification actions
- Adverse clinical privileges actions
- Adverse professional society membership actions
- Negative actions or findings by private accreditation organizations and peer-review organizations
- Health care-related criminal convictions and civil judgments
- Exclusions from participation in a Federal or state health care program (including Medicare and Medicaid exclusions)
- Other adjudicated actions or decisions[32]

Penalties for failing to report are stiff. Malpractice insurers are subject to fines of $23,331 per payment made.[33] Hospitals, health care entities, and professional societies that don't report when they should can be publicly reprimanded and lose certain immunities for civil liability.[34] A health plan that fails to report incurs a penalty of $39,811 for each adverse action not reported.[35]

Additionally, unlike the sex offender registry, which potential employers are not required to query, hospitals must ping the NPDB every time a physician applies for staff privileges and again every two years for those on its staff.[36]

Whereas a criminal defendant has a virtually unlimited right to appeal, practitioners have no such rights with regard to an NPDB report. The practitioner can only ever challenge the accuracy or reportability of the report.[37] The Department of Health and Human

---

[31] Van Tassel, *Blacklisted*, 33 *Cardozo L. Rev.* 2040.
[32] National Practitioner Data Bank, "What You Must Report to the NPDB," available at https://www.npdb.hrsa.gov/hcorg/whatYouMustReportToTheDataBank.jsp, last accessed August 24, 2023.
[33] *Id.*
[34] *Id.*
[35] *Id.*
[36] 42 USC § 11134–11137; U.S. Gen. Accounting Office, GAO-01-130, at 9.
[37] 45 CFR § 60.21(c)(2).

Services (HHS) does not ever "consider the merits or appropriateness of the action or the due process" provided to the practitioner.[38] So the HHS may correct a misspelling or make an adjustment to some language in the report, but to get them to void a report requires more than a showing of the merits. For the HSS to remove a report, it must not meet the criteria for reporting and have been errantly reported in the first place. As we will see in chapter 2, the criteria encompass physicians who have done nothing medically wrong.

Incredibly, not even a practitioner's death can remove the sting of the NPDB. If a settlement is made on behalf of a deceased doctor, the paying malpractice carrier is still under an obligation to report the payment, and the doctor's legacy is tarnished posthumously.[39]

While reading this section, I hope you have at least once considered how absurd it is that we find ourselves comparing the rights of physicians and criminals—two segments of our society that otherwise have almost no overlap.

Admittedly, criminal law, like medicine, does favor the (in this attorney's view) irrational use of vestigial Latin. And in criminal law, there is a Latin term, *mens rea*, which means "an evil purpose or mental culpability."[40] It is literally the intent to do harm, and virtually every crime requires proof of this "guilty mind."[41]

Physicians take an oath to "do no harm" and are actively pursuing careers whose main purpose is to help people, often to the detriment of the physicians' own health, family life, and otherwise. Criminals, on the other hand, by the very definition of the term, intentionally harm others to gain often-temporary position, possessions, or pleasure. Yet the former are left to fend for themselves with limited rights while the public funds the latter's defense to ensure their multitudinous rights are not infringed.

---

[38] *Id.* § 60.21(c)(1).
[39] Health Resources & Services Administration, "NPDB Guidebook," October 2018 at E-26, available at https://www.npdb.hrsa.gov/resources/NPDBGuidebook.pdf, last accessed January 4, 2023.
[40] *Staples v. United States*, 511 U.S. 600, 638, 114 S. Ct. 1793, 1813, 128 L. Ed. 2d 608 (1994).
[41] *Id.* at n. 25.

CHAPTER 2

Has the NPDB Had Its Intended Effect?

The NPDB was created in response to a perceived healthcare crisis and stories like those of Dr. Huffnagle, whom the system failed to detect, permitting him to continue his parade of harm. Remember, one of the explicit purposes of the HCQIA, the legislation that created the NPDB, was to "restrict the ability of incompetent physicians to move from State to State without disclosure or discovery of the physician's previous damaging or incompetent performance."[1]

Looking back on almost forty years of its existence, we have data to show that it casts too wide of a net—good doctors as well as bad are being reported. But is it at least catching all the bad doctors? The data suggests that it is not. Not even close.

We don't need to look far to see the post-NPDB-era Dr. Huffnagle. Dr. Christopher Duntch, a neurosurgeon out of Texas, is the most famous example. Dr. Duntch, nicknamed "Dr. Death," made Dr. Huffnagle's incompetence look mild in comparison. He has since been the subject of a popular podcast, an episode of *American Greed*, an episode of *License to Kill*, and a miniseries on the Peacock Streaming service starring Joshua Jackson, Alec Baldwin, and Christian Slater.

Dr. Duntch's reign of maiming and death began in 2011 at the Baylor Regional Medical Center in Plano, Texas and the Minimally Invasive Spine Institute in Dallas.[2]

---

[1] Health Care Quality Improvement Act, Pub. L. No. 99–660, tit. IV, 100 Stat. 3784 (1986) (codified as 42 U.S.C. 11101 et al.).
[2] Zajicek, J. "To Err Is Human, Unless You Are A Healthcare Provider," 4 *Belmont Health L.J.* 79, 92 (2020).

Baylor suspended his privileges, then later lifted the suspension.[3] When he resigned almost a year after beginning his employ, the hospital sent him on his way with a letter of recommendation.[4] He secured a position at the Dallas Medical Center, where out of three surgeries, he killed one patient and permanently disabled another.[5] After a fellow physician reported him to the Texas Medical Board, he performed another surgery that permanently damaged his patient's brain.[6] Finally, Texas suspended his medical license.[7]

All told, Dr. Duntch's gross incompetence killed two patients and maimed or paralyzed approximately twenty-five others over a period of two years.[8] An astounding thirty-three out of thirty-eight of his patients accused him of injuring them.[9]

Besides losing his license and being sued multiple times, he was eventually criminally prosecuted and convicted for multiple counts of aggravated assault.[10] He was sentenced to life in prison.[11] This was well into the era where the NPDB was supposed to catch and prevent this from happening.[12]

Part of the problem lies with the inconsistent reporting and enforcement of reporting. Despite the penalties for failing to report, only half of the nation's hospitals have ever reported a doctor to the NPDB.[13] Only one-third of Texas's hospitals have ever reported one of their doctors, and those that have rarely do it more than once.[14]

This may seem like a boon to practicing doctors. However, it creates lopsided results when hospitals fail to report their suspension of a doctor's privileges (they're required to report if the adverse action lasts longer than 30 days) but insurance companies regularly

---

[3] Zajiceck, "To Err is Human," 4 *Belmont Health L.J.* 93.
[4] *Id.*
[5] *Id.*
[6] *Id.*
[7] *Id.*
[8] Zajicek, "To Err is Human," 4 *Belmont Health L.J.* 92.
[9] *American Greed: The Real Dr. Death* (Television Production), United States: CNBC, February 1, 2021.
[10] Zajicek, "To Err is Human," 4 *Belmont Health L.J.* 93.
[11] *Id.*
[12] NPDB, you had one job …
[13] Eiser, T & Smith, M. February 10, 2020, *WFAA*, "'Dr. Death' Highlights Loopholes Putting Patients at Risk," available at https://www.wfaa.com/article/news/local/investigates/two-thirds-of-texas-hospitals-have-never-reported-a-bad-doctor-to-national-practitioner-databank-records-show/287-13d9f229-43e1-4c0c-8261-4933b09c55e8, last accessed October 19, 2022.
[14] *Id.*

make reports (they report when a payment is made for settlement of *any* amount, regardless of the reason).[15]

Although one case does not a pattern make, Dr. Death's reign of terror was beyond egregious. Worse than any of the handful of cases that prompted the creation of the NPDB in the first place. And yet the mechanisms in place to prevent this did not have their intended effect.

Getting Blacklisted – What Does It Mean?

Like the side effects of medication, having one's name reported to the NPDB affects different people differently. Many of my clients already have their names on the list for some reason or another. Some have noticed no ill effects. To others, the effect is detrimental. I know at least one doctor who was so angered by the injustice of it all that he left the practice of medicine altogether.[16]

Being a good-physician victim of the NPDB reporting system, while the same system misses the bad doctors, is like taking medication that does nothing to cure your ills but still comes with the nasty side effects.

If the NPDB were a warning label on medication (a medication that you have no choice but to take if you want to practice medicine), this is what it would say:

- May cause loss of hospital privileges
- May adversely affect credentialing
- May impact malpractice insurance rates or insurability
- May negatively impact job prospects or eliminate them altogether
- May affect health insurer's willingness to pay for your services
- May result in suspended or revoked medical license

For those relying on hospital staff privileges to produce income, being registered with the NPDB can be particularly injurious. As one Harvard professor put it, "the inability to use hospital facilities to treat patients so greatly curtails the physician's ability to practice his or her

---

[15] National Practitioner Data Bank, "What You Must Report to the NPDB," available at https://www.npdb.hrsa.gov/hcorg/whatYouMustReportToTheDataBank.jsp, last accessed August 24, 2023.
[16] He went to law school and became a lawyer. ☺

profession that it is, in effect, the end of that physician's career and his or her license to practice medicine is worthless."[17]

The state of California commissioned an expansive study to try to determine the reason reports to the NPDB in response to peer-review findings were low and declining. At least part of the reason for the reluctance to report related to the harshness of its consequences:

> Physicians who have been the subject of [a negative] report state that it is difficult or impossible to find a new position, their professional lives are ruined, other entities will not grant privileges even if they have fulfilled the terms of the discipline, and they spend years and hundreds of thousands of dollars in court trying to clear their professional names and reputations.[18]

Consider the cautionary tale of Dr. John Ulrich, a physician out of San Francisco. The facts are not disputed, and there is no legitimate claim that he did anything remotely negligent, dangerous, or wrong. Yet he was another victim of the senseless rules of the NPDB.[19]

Dr. Ulrich had been working for the Laguna Honda Hospital for almost 10 years when the hospital conducted a series of layoffs. Dr. Ulrich was not laid off, yet was vocal in protesting the decision of the San Francisco's Department of Health.[20] He objected to the layoffs because "they were an injustice to the patients by diminishing the physician-to-patient ratio as well as an injustice to the physicians being laid off."[21] At least some of those physicians were close to retirement, which Dr. Ulrich felt was wrong.[22] He became a leader in opposition to the layoffs, and several other staff members became outspoken against the decision to terminate an entire class of physicians.[23]

---

[17] Van Tassel, *Blacklisted,* 33 *Cardozo L. Rev.* 2057–58.
[18] Seago, JA. et al. "Comprehensive Study of Peer Review in California: Final Report," July 31, 2008, available at https://www.mbc.ca.gov/Download/Reports/peer-review.pdf, last accessed October 19, 2022.
[19] *Ulrich v. City & Cnty. of San Francisco,* 308 F.3d 968, 972 (9th Cir. 2002).
[20] *Id.*
[21] *Id.* (internal quotation marks omitted).
[22] *Id.* at 973.
[23] *Id.* at 972.

Shortly after his protests, and purportedly because of them, Dr. Ulrich received notice that he was being investigated for professional incompetence.[24]

Dr. Ulrich resigned in protest over the layoffs.[25]

Under the NPDB reporting requirements, a health care entity is required to report any adverse action if the entity "accepts the surrender of clinical privileges of a physician ... while the physician is under an investigation by the entity relating to possible incompetence or improper professional conduct."[26]

When Dr. Ulrich's attorney informed him of this fact, he attempted to rescind his resignation pending the outcome of the investigation, but the hospital refused.[27]

The hospital then sent the following adverse action report to the California Medical Board and the NPDB:

> Dr. Ulrich resigned from the Medical Staff, and relinquished his privileges, following receipt of a letter announcing the commencement of a formal investigation into his practice and professional conduct as a member of the Medical Staff and while caring for patients at the Hospital. That investigation was prompted as a result of concerns regarding apparent deficiencies in his practice and conduct spanning the full range of Hospital care, including incomplete diagnoses, inappropriate diagnostic and therapeutic orders, failures to accept appropriate responsibility for the course of patient treatment, and an overall absence of clear, effective management of hospitalizations. Dr. Ulrich submitted his resignation before this investigation had progressed to any findings or recommendations.[28]

Dr. Ulrich filed protests of the report, and after an investigation, the Medical Board of California (MBC) acquitted him of any wrongdoing, finding that there "was no departure in the standard of care."[29]

The HHS was notified of the MBC's findings, did not engage in an investigation of its own, and refused to void the report.[30] The hospital,

---

[24] *Id.*
[25] *Id.*
[26] 42 U.S.C. § 11133.
[27] *Ulrich*, 308 F.3d 973.
[28] *Id.*
[29] *Id.* at 973–74.
[30] *Id.* at 974.

which could have rescinded the report after the MBC made its finding, chose not to do so.[31] "According to the presidents of two medical associations in California, it [would] be virtually impossible for Dr. Ulrich to obtain employment as a practicing physician at any hospital in the country if the report on file with the NPDB [were] not voided."[32]

Dr. Ulrich sued, and at the district level, he lost. The district court refused to acknowledge Dr. Ulrich's argument that a negative NPDB report deprived him of liberty: "Every court to have addressed the issue has held that a wrongful report to the NPDB does not constitute a deprivation of a liberty or property interest that is protected by federal law.... '[T]he [NPDB] was not enacted for the benefit of physicians.' Given the ruling above, the Court need not reach this question."[33]

Dr. Ulrich appealed to the Ninth Circuit and received a more favorable ruling.[34] They disagreed with the district court, reversing its decision, and giving Dr. Ulrich the opportunity to prove his case again at the trial level.[35]

At the same time, Dr. Ulrich sued the hospital in state court seeking an injunction compelling the hospital to revoke the adverse action report.[36]

He had two lawsuits going at the same time: one in state court in hopes of getting his name removed from the NPDB, and one in federal court for money damages.

He lost the state court case because he could not prove that money damages would not be an adequate remedy.[37] In lay terms, the court was not convinced that removing his name from the NPDB would make him any more whole than if he prevailed in his civil case and was awarded money damages.

In federal court, he was required to take the case all the way to jury trial where, after hearing the facts, on June 8, 2004—six years after

---

[31] *Id.*
[32] *Id.*
[33] *Ulrich v. City & Cnty. of San Francisco*, No. C-99-05003 TEH, 2001 WL 253351, at *7 fn 4 (N.D. Cal. Mar. 9, 2001), aff'd in part, rev'd in part, 308 F.3d 968 (9th Cir. 2002).
[34] *Ulrich*, 308 F.3d at 986.
[35] *Id.*
[36] *Ulrich v. City & Cnty. of San Francisco*, No. A095219, 2002 WL 459778 (Cal. Ct. App. Mar. 26, 2002).
[37] *Id.*

the drama began—the jury awarded him $4.3 million in damages plus an undisclosed amount of costs.[38]

Few are the doctors, no matter the wrong, willing to take their case up and down trial and appellate courts in two different court systems. He lost more times than he won, and in the end, perhaps there is no better example of the damage and permanence of an NPDB report than this: Dr. Ulrich, whom no one can say did anything wrong, but was a victim of a vengeful hospital, was able to prove $4.3 million in damages, but could not get his name removed from the NPDB.

Dr. Ulrich's case is not an isolated one. Dr. Thomas Wieters, a surgeon out of Charleston, South Carolina, vocally criticized the care at Roper Hospital, concerned for the safety of his patients.[39] Dr. Wieters documented consistent examples of "failure to administer and document medications, incomplete nursing notes, [and] physician orders that weren't followed."

The hospital labeled him as "disruptive," issued a summary suspension, and reported him to the NPDB.

No one ever disputed his competence as a physician. After his suspension, 36 of his colleagues and 100 nurses signed a petition seeking his reinstatement. One doctor appointed to a committee to oversee the suspension stated that "No one, not even his detractors, has ever said he did not provide his patients with top care."

After two surprise inspections occurring after the suspension, Federal Medicare officials found evidence of the same kinds of problems Dr. Wieters was decrying. They found evidence of a fatal medication error, among others, and concluded that the conditions at Roper "pose an immediate and serious threat to the health and safety of patients." They promised to halt Medicare funding unless the hospital addressed the dangers outlined in their report.

Despite this vindication, Dr. Wieters could not find work in Charleston, having been blacklisted from two of the city's hospitals. He ended up having to work at a much smaller facility at 15–20% of his original pay.

---

[38] *Ulrich v. City & Cnty. of San Francisco*, No. C-99-05003-TEH, 2004 WL 1635542, at *1 (N.D. Cal. July 12, 2004).

[39] Twedt, S. October 26, 2003, *Pittsburgh Post-Gazette*, "The Cost of Courage: When Right Can Be Wrong," available at:
https://www.postgazette.com/news/nation/2003/10/27/The-Cost-of-Courage-When-right-can-be-wrong/stories/200310270027, last accessed October 19, 2022. All facts below relating to Dr. Weiters are from this article.

Even his remote practice dwindled. CIGNA Healthcare notified Dr. Wieters that it would no longer cover treatments he provided because of the NPDB report. It notified his patients that they should look for a new doctor.

He has sought work in North Carolina, San Francisco, Salt Lake City, Chicago, and Atlanta, and was told by physician recruiters everywhere that his registration with the NPDB made him far less hirable. "One recruiter told him the listing was as damaging as if he had been a convicted felon just released from prison. Another one asked [him], 'Have you ever considered employment outside the U.S.?'"[40]

Not everyone whose name gets reported is going to experience the same harmful effects. But unlike medication, which you can stop taking or replace with others with fewer side effects, medical practitioners have no choice but to keep taking the NPDB pill, no matter how hard it is to swallow or what its side effects are.

---

[40] *Id.*

CHAPTER 3

Keeping Your Name off the Data Bank: Prophylactic and Reactionary Measures

In my spare time, I like to build cabinets.[1] Yeah, I know, not what you were expecting at the beginning of this chapter. But the approach to cabinetmaking has some clear parallels to legal strategy.

My wife's office is on the second floor in a room where the ceiling is vaulted on either side. At the end of the room is a window overlooking the horses in the pasture across the street from our house.

She wanted some built-in cabinets on the wall with the window that would not obstruct her view. Before I began, I had to take measurements of the walls. Find the angle of the ceiling. Map out the location of the window, the wall outlet, and the ceiling vent. Then I created a rough drawing of the space with labeled measurements.

These became my constraining parameters. I had to work within them. The walls, ceiling, window, outlet, and vent were all in a fixed location. To move them would have required far more time and expertise than I had, and in some cases, city permits.[2]

I re-created these parameters in 3D software so I had a scale working model of the space. Then I drew the cabinets. Figured out where I wanted doors, how many, how to distribute the shelves, etc. I could do whatever I wanted if it was within the parameters fixed by the physical limitations of the room.

---

[1] Yes, I'm the only lawyer/cabinetmaker I know of.
[2] Don't get me started.

Once I had drawn up plans to satisfy the space constraints and fulfil my wife's vision, it was time to build. I cut the pieces, assembled them, and installed them. They fit perfectly, and they look great.

Legal strategizing is a similar process. First, we look to the law itself. Those are the parameters within which we must find a solution.

There is an entire field of study dedicated to the interpretation of statute, and in that field of study, there is one rule that takes precedence above all others: the way the law is written is presumed to be what the legislature intended, and courts interpreting the law will first consider the plain language of the statute, giving its terms their ordinary and accepted meaning.[3] Put another way, the words the legislature uses are the best indicator of what they intended in creating the statute. So that's where we start. With the unique combination of words that became the law.

But before we look at those codified words in the HCQIA that became the procedures surrounding the NPDB, let's go on a small (relevant) tangent related to the importance of word choice and punctuation(!) in drafting a statute. In this case, your reputation, even your livelihood, depends on the interpretation of the rules, but there have been real cases where a life hangs in the balance.

Consider the sad tale of Sir Roger Casement.

Hanged by an Inferred Comma

Sir Roger Casement was an Irish nationalist who, during the First World War, met with German officials in Berlin and New York in an attempt to contribute to an insurrection. He was brought back to Britain, tried for and convicted of high treason, and sentenced to death.[4]

On appeal, Casement called into question the statutory language defining treason. Any man who was "adherent to the king's enemies in his realm giving them aid and comfort in the realm or elsewhere..." was a traitor. Notably, there are no commas in this section of the statute.

The prosecution's position was that "or elsewhere" applied to both conditions—"adherent to the kings enemies" and "giving them aid and

---

[3] *State v. Roman-Rosado*, 462 N.J. Super. 183, 197, 225 A.3d 544, 552 (App. Div. 2020), aff'd as modified sub nom. State v. Carter, 247 N.J. 488, 255 A.3d 1139 (2021)

[4] Parry, ZB. July 16, 2014, *Las Vegas Tribune*, "Verdicts and Judgments: When Life or Death Hangs on a Comma."

comfort"—so the statute applied to all men "adherent to the king's enemies" anywhere and "giving them aid and comfort" anywhere.

Casement argued, however, that the prosecution was reading the statute as though there were a comma before the term "or elsewhere." He argued that a better reading of the statute was that his actions weren't treacherous because he had been "adherent to the king's enemies" outside the king's realm, whereas a traitor had to have both been "adherent to the king's enemies in his realm" and "giv[en] them aid and comfort" anywhere.

The court apparently found Casement's argument persuasive because instead of relying on the punctuation of the version of the statute before it, two of the judges went to inspect the original copy of the statute, looking for the comma that could justify the death sentence meted out by the lower court.

Although they found no comma before "or elsewhere," they found the next-best thing—a virgule (a slash [/], the comma's predecessor)—right where they needed it to be. However, there was some question as to whether the mark was a genuine virgule or just a permanent shadow created from a crease resulting from six centuries of folding and unfolding of the paper statute. Regardless, the judges had found their justification and thus inferred the comma that resulted in the hanging of Sir Roger Casement.

This case serves to illustrate the importance of a statute's language. And the lengths to which courts will go to interpret them a certain way.

With that as a preface, let's dive into the various statutes, regulations, and official publications that form the body of law related to the NPDB and its reporting requirements. First stop: the HCQIA itself.

What does the statute say? How does it say it? Perhaps more importantly, what does it leave unsaid? Those will be the walls, ceilings, and other parameters that define the space within which we have to work. With that, we can draw up a plan. Then we build.

In the last chapter, we looked at the current form of the HCQIA and also at some of its history—details that don't come through from reading the statute. We wanted to get a complete picture of what it requires and what it doesn't. But now we want to scrutinize the words. Take precise measurements.

Let's look at the reporting requirement that applies to malpractice insurance companies. Here it is verbatim:

Each entity (including an insurance company) which makes payment under a policy of insurance, self-insurance, or otherwise in settlement (or partial settlement) of, or in satisfaction of a judgment in, a medical malpractice action or claim shall report, in accordance with section 11134 of this title, information respecting the payment and circumstances thereof.[5]

Ok. So now we have our parameters. Whatever we do, we have to operate within these black-and-white rules the legislature has enacted. We must operate within the letter of the law.

Bear with me here as I undergo the legal analysis. Understanding how doctors end up on the list will inform our approach to ensure you aren't an unwitting addition and victim to the attendant reputational and financial damage.

Who Has to Report Payments?

The first thing we're going to look at is who is subject to the reporting requirement. To whom does the HCQIA apply? And significantly, to whom does it not apply?

The words of the statute call out "each entity."[6] So it only applies to entities, right? This is an instance where what the statute says is as important as what it doesn't say.

If it singles out entities making payments for a malpractice claim, then it stands to reason that it doesn't apply to non-entities, like individuals.

Indeed, if a doctor pays a settlement out of their own pocket, eschewing indemnity protection from the insurer, that's non-reportable.[7]

---

[5] 42 U.S.C. § 11131(a). There are other sections that require medical boards and health care entities to report under other circumstances.

[6] We have to ignore the fact that the legislators meant the phrase "which makes payment ..." as a defining clause—designating which specific insurers are beholden to the statute—and so erred in their word choice. They should have said "insurance company *that* makes payment," not "insurance company *which* makes payment," though that's a grammatical exploitation I will leave for others to make.

[7] National Practitioner Data Bank, April 14, 2021, "Medical Malpractice Payments Reporting Requirements Teleconference," available at

https://www.npdb.hrsa.gov/community_n_education/webcasts/medicalMalpracticeTeleconference.jsp, last accessed August 24, 2023.

comfort"—so the statute applied to all men "adherent to the king's enemies" anywhere and "giving them aid and comfort" anywhere.

Casement argued, however, that the prosecution was reading the statute as though there were a comma before the term "or elsewhere." He argued that a better reading of the statute was that his actions weren't treacherous because he had been "adherent to the king's enemies" outside the king's realm, whereas a traitor had to have both been "adherent to the king's enemies in his realm" and "giv[en] them aid and comfort" anywhere.

The court apparently found Casement's argument persuasive because instead of relying on the punctuation of the version of the statute before it, two of the judges went to inspect the original copy of the statute, looking for the comma that could justify the death sentence meted out by the lower court.

Although they found no comma before "or elsewhere," they found the next-best thing—a virgule (a slash [/], the comma's predecessor)—right where they needed it to be. However, there was some question as to whether the mark was a genuine virgule or just a permanent shadow created from a crease resulting from six centuries of folding and unfolding of the paper statute. Regardless, the judges had found their justification and thus inferred the comma that resulted in the hanging of Sir Roger Casement.

This case serves to illustrate the importance of a statute's language. And the lengths to which courts will go to interpret them a certain way.

With that as a preface, let's dive into the various statutes, regulations, and official publications that form the body of law related to the NPDB and its reporting requirements. First stop: the HCQIA itself.

What does the statute say? How does it say it? Perhaps more importantly, what does it leave unsaid? Those will be the walls, ceilings, and other parameters that define the space within which we have to work. With that, we can draw up a plan. Then we build.

In the last chapter, we looked at the current form of the HCQIA and also at some of its history—details that don't come through from reading the statute. We wanted to get a complete picture of what it requires and what it doesn't. But now we want to scrutinize the words. Take precise measurements.

Let's look at the reporting requirement that applies to malpractice insurance companies. Here it is verbatim:

Each entity (including an insurance company) which makes payment under a policy of insurance, self-insurance, or otherwise in settlement (or partial settlement) of, or in satisfaction of a judgment in, a medical malpractice action or claim shall report, in accordance with section 11134 of this title, information respecting the payment and circumstances thereof.[5]

Ok. So now we have our parameters. Whatever we do, we have to operate within these black-and-white rules the legislature has enacted. We must operate within the letter of the law.

Bear with me here as I undergo the legal analysis. Understanding how doctors end up on the list will inform our approach to ensure you aren't an unwitting addition and victim to the attendant reputational and financial damage.

Who Has to Report Payments?

The first thing we're going to look at is who is subject to the reporting requirement. To whom does the HCQIA apply? And significantly, to whom does it not apply?

The words of the statute call out "each entity."[6] So it only applies to entities, right? This is an instance where what the statute says is as important as what it doesn't say.

If it singles out entities making payments for a malpractice claim, then it stands to reason that it doesn't apply to non-entities, like individuals.

Indeed, if a doctor pays a settlement out of their own pocket, eschewing indemnity protection from the insurer, that's non-reportable.[7]

---

[5] 42 U.S.C. § 11131(a). There are other sections that require medical boards and health care entities to report under other circumstances.

[6] We have to ignore the fact that the legislators meant the phrase "which makes payment ..." as a defining clause—designating which specific insurers are beholden to the statute—and so erred in their word choice. They should have said "insurance company *that* makes payment," not "insurance company *which* makes payment," though that's a grammatical exploitation I will leave for others to make.

[7] National Practitioner Data Bank, April 14, 2021, "Medical Malpractice Payments Reporting Requirements Teleconference," available at
https://www.npdb.hrsa.gov/community_n_education/webcasts/medicalMalpracticeTeleconference.jsp, last accessed August 24, 2023.

But, like every other claim I make in this book, you don't have to take my word for it. (That's what all those footnotes are for.) This issue came before a federal appeals court in Washington, D.C. in 1993. The court's decision was unambiguous (and illustrates the grammatical nuance that goes into interpreting a statute):

> The Health Care Act reveals unmistakably that Congress did not intend to encompass any individual doctor or dentist as an "entity" that must report to the National Practitioner Data Bank. The Act does not define "entity," but the term as used in the Act refers uniformly to groups and organizations. Whenever the Act discusses individual persons, words such as "physician," "doctor," "dental surgeon," "individual," and "person" are consistently employed. Moreover, the phrase "person *or* entity" appears elsewhere in the Act, *see* 42 U.S.C. § 11137(c) (emphasis added), which would be nonsensical if "entity" already encompassed "person." Thus, all of the textual evidence points in one direction: Congress did not intend the term "entity" to encompass individual practitioners.[8]

In a win for practitioners, the NPDB, in response to this case, "removed previously submitted reports on medical malpractice payments made by individuals for their own benefit."[9] This remains the rule today.

In my days as a medical malpractice attorney representing plaintiff patients, doctors paying their own settlements was common. If the settlement were somewhere south of $50,000, typically, the doctor would pay using their own money.

Seems absurd, right? The doctor is spending thousands of dollars in insurance premiums, and the purpose of that insurance is to make those payments so the doctor doesn't have to use their own money. Yet the doctor is choosing to turn down coverage and write a personal check.

Incredibly, these doctors were paying up to $50,000 to keep their names off the NPDB.[10]

---

[8] *Am. Dental Ass'n v. Shalala*, 3 F.3d 445, 446–47 (D.C. Cir. 1993).
[9] National Practitioner Data Bank, "Reporting Medical Malpractice Payments," available at https://www.npdb.hrsa.gov/guidebook/EMMPR.jsp, last accessed August 24, 2023.
[10] That shouldn't be that shocking after hearing the stories of the doctors in the last chapter who spent hundreds of thousands of dollars in litigation trying to get their names off the list.

As far as planning ahead to give yourself options in a lawsuit, it's not ideal. In fact, if you don't plan beforehand, it's about the only option you have if you want to keep your name off the list. That or win your case completely.

Still, ideal or not, we've now identified one exception to the malpractice-settlements-are-reportable rule in the first two words of the reporting statute. Let's look for others.

What Constitutes a Malpractice Action or Claim?

Now that we've identified who is responsible for submitting the reports, let's look at what triggers the mandatory reporting.

The statute, like virtually every statute I've ever analyzed, eschews plain English in favor of complicated legalese with far too many commas.[11] For some reason, legislative drafters like paragraph-long sentences. This one is no exception. The entire paragraph is a 53-word sentence. But that's what we have to work with, so let's break it down.

Who: [Any] entity ... [that] makes payment

So it's any entity. Not an individual. Right. We covered that.

Is there a minimum payment amount? It may surprise you to know that there is not. The statute says it all: "makes payment." Although some state boards have a minimum payment threshold for their reporting requirement,[12] the NPDB does not. It was considered and discussed in hearings with lawmakers, but they declined to place any sort of minimum threshold.[13] The guidebook expands on what's already clear in the statute: "The amount of payment is irrelevant; there is no de minimis exception."[14]

---

[11] I wrote six riveting pages about the first paragraph of the statute that gave birth to the 401k, 26 U.S.C. 401(k). Spoiler alert: in the first sentence, it contains "definitional references to five different statutes in three different places, a confusing double negative, and circular definitions." *See* Parry, Z. *Unshackled: How to Escape the Chains of Conventional Wisdom that Keep You Poor*, (Boss Media: New York, 2020) 25–31.

[12] California, for example, only requires settlements or judgments of over $30,000 to be reported. California Business & Professions Code § 801.01.

[13] Hearings on H.R. 5110: Before the Subcomm. on Health and the Environment of the House Comm. on Energy and Commerce, 99th Cong., 2d Sess. 99-660, 14 & 373.

[14] HRSA, "NPDB Guidebook," October 2018, at E-19

What kind of payment? Here the grammar trips us up a bit. Syntax suggests an absurd interpretation of the statute, and in particular, which payments this phrase applies to: "in settlement ... of, or in satisfaction of a judgment in, a medical malpractice action or claim."

Does it apply only to payments made "otherwise" as the grammar suggests? If so, it would look like this:

A payment
(1) under a policy of insurance,
(2) [under a policy of] self-insurance, or
(3) otherwise in settlement (or partial settlement) of, or in satisfaction of a judgment in, a medical malpractice action or claim

Because there is no comma after "otherwise," and because there is a comma between "in" and "a medical malpractice action or claim," grammatically we have to put everything in paragraph (3) together.[15]

This interpretation would mean that any time any entity makes an insurance payment in any context, it would have to be reported.

However, even though the syntax of the sentence suggests this interpretation, we know that if a doctor gets into a car accident, and the car insurance makes a payment, that doesn't require a report. So we can't interpret it the way it was written.

That's another canon of statutory interpretation: if an otherwise unambiguous statute would lead to absurd results, the statute must be interpreted contrary to its plain language.[16]

Grammar and syntax aside,[17] it seems the legislature intended the statute to be read more like this:

---

[15] If you are listening to this book rather than reading it, please accept my apologies in advance. It can't be easy to follow this part. Take some consolation in the fact that seeing it doesn't make it much easier.

[16] Manning, JF. "The Absurdity Doctrine," 116 Harv. L. Rev. 2387, 2389 (2003); see e.g., *Clinton v. City of New York*, 524 U.S. 417, 429 (1998); *Pub. Citizen v. U.S. Dep't of Justice*, 491 U.S. 440, 454-55 (1989); *Jackson v. Lykes Bros. S.S. Co.*, 386 U.S. 731, 735 (1967); *United States v. Brown*, 333 U.S. 18, 27 (1948); *Armstrong Paint & Varnish Works v. Nu-Enamel Corp.*, 305 U.S. 315, 333 (1938); *Sorrells v. United States*, 287 U.S. 435, 447–49 (1932); *United States v. Katz*, 271 U.S. 354, 362 (1926); *Hawaii v. Mankichi*, 190 U.S. 197, 213–14 (1903); *Church of the Holy Trinity v. United States*, 143 U.S. 457, 465, 472 (1892); *Kirby*, 74 U.S. (7 Wall.) at 487.

[17] It is unfortunate that in interpreting statutes written by professional law drafters who understand the importance of every comma, when scrutinizing their work product, we so often have to set grammar and syntax aside to get at the real meaning behind the words.

A payment
  (1) under a policy of insurance,
  (2) [under a policy of] self-insurance, or
  (3) otherwise
—[if any of the above is paid] in settlement (or partial settlement) of, or in satisfaction of a judgment in, a medical malpractice action or claim

Like the judiciary in the case of Sir Roger Casement, we're inferring a comma between "otherwise" and "in settlement," such that any payment made by an entity, whether through insurance or otherwise, to satisfy a medical malpractice claim, is reportable.

So can we find some room in the HCQIA here for an exception to the reporting requirement?

The word "otherwise" makes the payment provision broad. The money doesn't have to come from insurance. It's a payment under insurance "or otherwise." Nothing to see there.

The last line is broad, too. There are only two reasons for a doctor to make a payment to a patient through insurance: (1) voluntarily, which is a settlement, and (2) because of a judgment issued by a judge or jury. So regardless of the outcome of the case, whether it was voluntarily settled or the doctor lost, the payment counts. The only other potential outcome would be if the doctor wins the case, in which case there is no report anyway. But what exactly constitutes a settlement? How do we know what is "in settlement of" a malpractice action or claim?

Turns out this is pretty important for reporting purposes. And although we have to look for secondary sources for this one (the statute itself is not sufficiently clear), the NPDB has clarified that for a payment to be "in settlement" of a medical malpractice claim or action, it has to compensate the plaintiff for their injuries:

> Reportable medical malpractice payments are limited to exchanges of money and must be the result of a written complaint or claim demanding monetary payment for damages relating to medical care. These fees, known as loss adjustment expenses (LAEs), refer to expenses other than those in compensation of injuries, such as attorney fees, billable hours, copying costs, expert witness fees, and deposition and transcript costs. Reimbursement of these fees [is] not

reportable to the NPDB in and of [itself]. LAEs should only be reported to the NPDB if they are included in a medical malpractice settlement.[18]

I had one smaller case where this exception was the key to settlement. The defense was willing to pay every dime of all costs and expenses, including my fees, in exchange for release, and the plaintiff agreed. Case settled, no report. In situations like this, the plaintiff is willing to go along with a settlement just for costs because they can often negotiate the medical bills, getting them reduced, in which case, the plaintiff can keep the difference and still gets money in their pockets.

If you're in this position and finding that offering fees and costs is not quite enough to induce plaintiff to settle, you could also offer to waive any payments on medical bills the plaintiff may still owe you for your services. That doesn't count as "payment," so it's not reportable, either.[19]

Presto! We've found our second exception to the malpractice-settlements-are-reportable rule.

Let's look again at that last phrase of the statute's sentence/paragraph. Payments made in settlement of or in satisfaction of a judgment in "a medical malpractice action or claim."

Do you see it? We have something to work with here. And here comes another important lesson about statutory interpretation: definitions matter.

Recall in the 1993 D.C. case that the court called out Congress for not defining the term "entity." The court had to look at how the word was used and infer its definition. Since the inferred meaning didn't encompass individuals, the statute didn't apply to payments made by individuals.

It is for this reason that many statutes have an entire section devoted to "definitions." Congress wants to make sure its meaning is clear. The HCQIA is no exception. Title 42, Chapter 117, Subchapter III, Section 11151 is called "Definitions," and defines some of the terms used in the HCQIA (but not "entity").[20]

---

[18] U.S. Department of Health & Human Services, NPDB Insights, "Is It Reportable?" available at https://www.npdb.hrsa.gov/enews/May2016Insights.jsp#Article2, last accessed August 24, 2023.
[19] 45 CFR § 60.7(a).
[20] 42 U.S.C. § 11151.

So what about the term "medical malpractice action or claim"? Yep, it's defined:

> The term "medical malpractice action or claim" means a written claim or demand for payment based on a health care provider's furnishing (or failure to furnish) health care services, and includes the filing of a cause of action, based on the law of tort, brought in any court of any State or the United States seeking monetary damages.[21]

Yes. We can work with that. Payments made by an insurance company in response to the filing of a cause of action—meaning active litigation—apply. And so do written claims or demands "for payment" based on treatment provided.

Can you see the gap there created by what the legislature didn't say?

Imagine the entire world of claims—every possible way a patient could make a claim. Is there anything other than demanding money or suing you? You bet.

How about if they don't sue you, but they demand something other than payment? How about if they make an oral demand for payment?

Bingo.

If you haven't been sued yet, and no written demand for payment has been made, your insurance company can pay money on your behalf, in response to a complaint about the medical treatment you provided (or failed to provide), and that's not reportable because the patient's action did not qualify as a "medical malpractice action or claim."

Awesome, right?

Well, it would be if the patient knew about it. Once the patient demands money (which they're almost always going to do) or sues you (if it happens, it usually follows your denial of their demand for money), you're now in the position where you have only three choices, and none of them is good: (1) settle the case with insurance money and have your name reported to the NPDB, (2) settle the case with your own money to keep your name off the list, or (3) take it all the way to trial and hope you win.

So what can we do about it?

---

[21] *Id.* § 11151(7).

We'll answer that question in a few pages. For now, you'll have to be satisfied knowing we've now found a third exception to the NPDB reporting requirement.

What About the Report Itself?

Let's continue to scrutinize the requirement. Remember, once the legislature puts their intent into writing, we all have to follow it, including the legislature. Because their words are presumed to capture their intent.

The legislature chose the word "entity" and defined "medical malpractice action or claim" to exclude oral demands for payment and nonmonetary written demands, so we presume that's what they intended, and that's the standard courts are holding us to.

In the previous section we analyzed 53 words and found three exceptions. Most of the HCQIA's words are intentionally broad, so there isn't much else there we can use. But what about the content of the report itself? Let's turn to the statute again, which describes the information in the report to the NPDB (whereas earlier we looked at the requirement to report):

(b) Information to be reported

The information to be reported under subsection (a)[that's the 53-word paragraph sentence we just analyzed] includes—

(1) the name of any physician or licensed health care practitioner for whose benefit the payment is made,

(2) the amount of the payment,

(3) the name (if known) of any hospital with which the physician or practitioner is affiliated or associated,

(4) a description of the acts or omissions and injuries or illnesses upon which the action or claim was based, and

(5) such other information as the Secretary determines is required for appropriate interpretation of information reported under this section.[22]

Seems straightforward enough. Once an entity makes a payment in settlement or judgment of a medical malpractice action or claim, that entity now must send the NPDB a report that includes the information above.

The gap here is harder to spot. It seems obvious that the name of the doctor would be included in the report, but there's that qualifying provision after that makes all the difference. The one that says, "for whose benefit the payment is made."

"For whose benefit the payment is made." There is an entire world of opportunity in that one phrase.

I will never accuse legislative drafters of being good writers. And why would they need to be? It's only the entire population of citizens, residents, and visitors to the United States—hundreds of millions of people—that are obliged follow the laws they write.[23]

The inclusion of the physician's name in the details of what should be in the report highlights a glaring error in the mandatory reporting provision earlier in the statute: it doesn't mention the *doctor* at all.

In a statute designed "to restrict the ability of incompetent physicians to move from State to State without disclosure or discovery of the physician's previous damaging or incompetent performance,"[24] it's odd that the mandatory reporting section doesn't mention "physicians" or "licensed medical practitioners" at all.

In simple terms, the mandatory reporting statute says that any entity making a payment in response to a medical malpractice or claim must submit a report. Not that any payment made in response to a claim *against a doctor* requires a report.

Reading the statute's reporting requirement, you would think the doctor irrelevant—that it's just the payment that matters. But then when it comes time to create the report, the doctor becomes relevant again. You probably don't see it yet, but this divergence between the two requirements becomes significant. Let me explain.

Normally I don't like the term loophole. It has negative connotations. Almost like people using the "loophole" are taking advantage of a poorly written rule in a way that was never intended. I

---

[22] *Id.* § 11131(b).
[23] Is sarcasm appropriate in a legal book? It's my book, and I say that it is.
[24] 42 U.S.C. § 11101(2).

don't think these first three exceptions we've identified are loopholes—that the rule doesn't apply to individuals, to payments of costs and fees only, or to settlements in response to oral demands or written demands for something other than payment. We just read the statute, drew lines where the statute said to draw them, then looked at what was left outside the lines.

This one, though, does not seem to have been intended.

Still don't see it?

It's subtle, but once you see it, you'll realize it's big enough a train could go through it. One carrying thousands of doctors.

Here's the scenario: the patient sues a hospital, clinic, or other entity. The entity has insurance, and in response to the lawsuit, the insurance company settles the case. Because the mandatory reporting requirements are triggered, the insurance company now has to put a report together.

The insurance company's representative opens their letterhead and types out the top portions and gets to the salutation then references the statute to make sure everything required is included.

They get to the first requirement: "the name of any physician or licensed health care practitioner for whose benefit the payment is made."

They aren't sure what to put. Payment wasn't made on behalf of a physician or licensed practitioner. It wasn't made on behalf of a person at all. Their options are to either send a report devoid of the required information, or not send a report at all.

Can you see where we're going here?

It seems reasonable that the report would require the physician's name. The medical blacklist wouldn't be much of a list if it didn't have names on it. But if the report requires the name of the person on whose behalf payment was made, and the payment made is not on behalf of any person, then does that obviate the need to report?

Let's see if the statutory definitions lend any aid.

Congress had the foresight to define both "physician" and "licensed health care practitioner":

> The term "physician" means a doctor of medicine or osteopathy or a doctor of dental surgery or medical dentistry legally authorized to practice medicine and surgery or dentistry by a

State (or any individual who, without authority holds himself or herself out to be so authorized).[25]

The terms "licensed health care practitioner" and "practitioner" mean, with respect to a State, an individual (other than a physician) who is licensed or otherwise authorized by the State to provide health care services.[26]

Based on these definitions, there seems to be little doubt that Congress intended the terms to include only individuals. People. Which makes sense. The NPDB is a blacklist of doctors, not of hospitals or other organizations.[27]

Let's consider the practical implications of this language: if an insurance company makes a payment on behalf of an entity or group, rather than an individual practitioner, that payment does not trigger the mandatory reporting requirement, or if it does, the report that goes out won't have any physician's name on it. Both result in the same effect: no practitioner's name goes on the list.

But what about a private practice or clinic that is the physician? What if you're the only licensed practitioner in your "group"? That's where the good news ends. Whether or not the HHS intended this "loophole," they've since embraced it.

Here's the official word, straight from the NPDB's website:

Medical malpractice payments made solely for the benefit of a corporation—such as a clinic, group practice, or hospital—should not be reported to the NPDB. A payment made for the benefit of a professional corporation or other business entity that consists of only a sole practitioner must be reported if the payment was made by the entity rather than by the sole practitioner out of personal funds.[28]

---

[25] *Id.* § 11151(8).
[26] *Id.* § 11151(6).
[27] HRSA, "NPDB Guidebook," October 2018, at E-19 ("[A malpractice report] is submitted on a particular health care practitioner, not an organization.").
[28] NPDB, "Reporting Medical Malpractice Payments," available at https://www.npdb.hrsa.gov/guidebook/EMMPR.jsp; *see also* HRSA, "NPDB Guidebook," October 2018, at E-16 ("A payment made as a result of a suit or claim solely against an entity (for example, a hospital, clinic, or group practice) that does not identify as an individual practitioner should not be reported to the NPDB.")

And so we have found exception number four: if an otherwise reportable payment is made on behalf of anything other than an individual physician or licensed medical practitioner, a complete report (one that includes the physician's name) is impossible and therefore unnecessary (but only in certain circumstances, as we'll discuss in the next chapter).

CHAPTER 4

How Do These Exceptions Benefit the Practitioner?

We've identified four narrow circumstances in which a payment made in response to a medical malpractice claim is not reportable. One requires the doctor to use personal funds, one is a settlement made only for loss adjustment expenses, the third relies on the patient to make demands orally or for something other than payment, and the fourth only applies when the payment is not made on behalf of the doctor. So how does this help? These circumstances seem narrow enough that they're rarely going to apply, or when they do—like when the doctor uses personal money to settle a case—the solution is hardly better than the problem.

Setting aside the use-of-personal-funds exception (that's not going to be part of any good plan, so let's just call it a last-resort option), there are things almost any practitioner can do to mitigate their risk and give themselves the best options for avoiding an NPDB report with their name on it.

You've Got Patient Contracts: Use Them!

I have never been to a doctor's office where I didn't have to sign far more paperwork than I thought strictly necessary. My favorite medical paperwork memory[1] happened when I went in for my first appointment with an ophthalmologist in preparation for LASIK.

I don't know if this was standard procedure for the office, but they dilated my eyes before giving me the paperwork. When they handed me the clipboard, my vision was so blurry the only indication I had that there was writing on the paper was a slight gray hue, where a blank paper would have been white.[2]

I looked up towards what I thought was the face of the member of the medical staff who handed me the clipboard and made the most incredulous face I could muster. She didn't say anything, and I couldn't read her expression to tell if she noticed the incredulity I was broadcasting, so I spoke. "I can't see this."

"Oh!" She said, seemingly embarrassed. "That's right." Then she reached out and grabbed my hand holding the pen and moved it towards the bottom of the paper. "That's where the signature line is. Sorry about that."

"Are you asking me to agree to terms on a document I can't see?"

"Do you want me to read it to you?" She asked, her tone letting me know it would be unreasonable for me to say yes.

"If you want me to sign it, I need to know what it is," I said.

"Well, this first form confirms that we provided you with a statement of your right to confidentiality of your medical information."

"Ok, that seems simple enough. Where is that statement?"

"We have one in our files. Did you want me to get you one?"

"I don't particularly want one, no. But I am also not going to attest in writing that you gave me one if you didn't give me one. So I guess it's up to you whether you want me to sign this."

The rest of the exchange was more of the same.[3] I couldn't see her, but I feel like the tone of her voice conveyed more disdain for my questions than anything her face could have told me anyway.

---

[1] I didn't know that was a thing until I wrote that sentence.
[2] I kid you not, at that moment, a scene from *Return of the Jedi* flashed before my malfunctioning eyes. Han Solo, who had been blind from hibernation sickness after having spent the time between *The Empire Strikes Back* and *Return of the Jedi* encased in carbonite, was taken from the dungeons of Jabba's Palace out to the unforgiving glare of Tatooine's twin sons. He turned to Luke and said, "I think my eyes are getting better. Instead of a big dark blur, I see a big light blur."
[3] Was I a jerk in that situation? Sometimes it is hard for me to tell.

I'm a lawyer, so I understand what it means to sign a contract.[4] And that's the point. What that contract says matters. And now that we've discovered the operating parameters of the NPDB reporting requirement, why not put that knowledge to good use?

While you're getting your patients to sign the HIPAA release, the informed consent, the insurance forms, and to fill out family history, let's also educate them as to the procedure for bringing a claim.

Your relationship with the patient is one based on contract, right? It's a transaction. You agree to provide medical care, and they agree to pay you. It's all right there in that paperwork they fill out when they become your patient.[5]

You're the one who gets to say what's in that contract. Patients don't come in with their own contracts. They sign yours.

So let's put a mediation provision in your new-patient paperwork. If the attorney who prepared your patient documents was even halfway decent, you probably already have a mediation provision. They're very common in all sorts of contracts, not just doctor-patient contracts.

In case you're not familiar, mediation is a settlement process. Typically the parties meet at a neutral location, like a mediator's office. They usually occupy separate rooms while the mediator shuttles back and forth, conveying the respective positions and attempting to get the parties to see each other's perspectives, coaching them about what they can expect if they don't reach an agreement, and trying to get them to resolve the matter.

The purpose of most mediation clauses is to save time and money. And it certainly takes far less of both to spend a few hours hashing out an agreement than to spend years hiring experts, taking depositions, and otherwise building a case for trial.

A mediation provision for a patient typically says something like this:

> If a dispute arises between Patient and Doctor, the Parties agree that they will first engage in mediation, and that both Parties will participate in good faith. Costs related to mediation

---

[4] I also understood that had I just said nothing and signed where indicated, and they had later tried to enforce the contract against me, they would have faced some serious hurdles when faced with my procedural unconscionability arguments. I used that experience as an example in the Contracts class I taught at UNLV.

[5] Or at least it should be. Now might be a good time to go take another look at your new patient paperwork and make sure it includes everything you want it to.

will be split equally between the Parties. Notwithstanding the foregoing, the Parties retain their right to proceed to arbitration or litigation.

That's a smart option, but it isn't complete. Not now that we know what we know about NPDB reporting.

If that's the only agreement you have, it may save you time and your malpractice insurer money, but the settlement resulting from mediation will likely still be reportable. Why? Because when Congress defined "medical malpractice action or claim," that included any "written claim or demand for payment." And what is almost every attorney going to do to initiate mediation? Send you a demand letter. And that demand letter is going to have a dollar figure in it. That's all it takes. Now the payment made at mediation is reportable. How likely is it now that you're going to settle? Mediation under those circumstances is a waste of time if it is just going to result in your name on the NPDB.

But what if in your mediation agreement you make one subtle change? The patient is going to contractually agree that if a dispute arises, they will not make any demand for *payment*, but rather make a demand for *mediation*.

If in the demand letter, they ask to mediate, but they do not make any claim or demand for payment, they have not triggered the mandatory NPDB reporting.

Then when you show up to mediation, they can relay oral demands for payment all day long.[6] And if it's a case you want to settle, do it. It isn't reportable because the demand for payment was not in writing, and therefore it didn't qualify as a "medical malpractice action or claim." And without that, there is no obligation to report.

It seems a little bit silly when you think about it. The reporting doesn't hinge on how bad the patient may have been hurt. It doesn't come down to how far outside the standard of care your treatment might have been. In this case, it comes down to whether the patient wrote the dollar sign down.

Maybe it is silly. I don't know. But the law is a series of words. And words have meaning. Especially, apparently, if they're written down.

---

[6] And mediation often takes all day.

The Patient Doesn't Have to Follow the Contract for You to Be Protected

Suppose you do integrate such a mediation agreement into your practice. It requires, as a condition to filing a lawsuit, that mediation be attempted. And suppose further that your patient sues you before attempting mediation. Are you now back in a position where a settlement will result in an NPDB report? Yes, you are. But that's ok. You wouldn't want to settle. Because now you've got all the leverage you need to win your case.

Even if you have all your patients sign the agreement, the reality is, most are not going to read it, they're certainly not going to keep a copy of it, and even if they do read it, by the time they're wanting to come after you, they're not going to remember it.

But if they want to make a claim against you, their attorney is going to want to see their medical records, and those records are going to include the mediation agreement.

Then one of two things will happen. Either (1) the attorney reads it and points out to the patient that they have to attempt mediation before they sue, or (2) they sue anyway, either because the attorney didn't read it or because they're so close to the statute of limitations that they can't wait any longer.

Either way, you are in a good position.

If they follow the instructions and demand mediation, you are in a great position. You can choose to settle, in which case your name isn't reported because the mediation and settlement hasn't amounted to a "medical malpractice action or claim." Or, if you choose not to settle, then it goes to a lawsuit where you can prove your case.

On the other hand, if they do not follow the directions, and they go straight to a lawsuit, you're still in a great position. Those instructions they didn't follow? They aren't just suggestions. They are contractually required. The contract binds them as strongly as the law does. And if they don't follow the contractual and procedural prerequisites to filing a lawsuit, then they don't get to pursue their lawsuit.

That's when your attorney files a motion to dismiss, and Exhibit 1 is going to be the mediation agreement with their signature on it. No mediation, no lawsuit. Lawsuit dismissed.

If this case is like so many other cases, and it is filed on the eve of the statute of limitations expiring, then they just lost their case. Permanently.

That's one paragraph in your new-patient paperwork doing all that heavy lifting. One paragraph specifically crafted to take advantage of Congress' definition of "medical malpractice action or claim."

If Only Individual Practitioners Get Reported, Not Groups, then Become a Group!

That last exception we found—that only payments on behalf of individuals are reportable—is what has become known as the Corporate Shield. It is the most well-known reporting exception, and although it isn't exactly clear from the statute itself, it is acknowledged by the NPDB on its website and in its published guidebook.[7]

Settlement on behalf of a sole practitioner is reportable if in response to a written complaint or claim for a failure to provide health care services, even if a professional corporation or other entity composed of a sole practitioner makes the payment for the benefit of a named practitioner.[8] But a payment made on behalf of a clinic, group practice, or hospital is not reportable if other requirements are met.[9]

So the distinction between the individual and the clinic, group practice, or hospital is important.

Again, we're going to turn to the definitions for help.

Recall that practitioners and physicians are both defined as "individuals."[10] The term "health care entity" is defined in two different places, in the United States Code[11] (Congressional bills that are codified into statute make their way there) and the Code of Federal Regulations[12] (rules propagated by federal agencies, in this case, the HHS).

The two rulemaking bodies have slightly different definitions of the same terms used in the same context (related to the NPDB), but what's important for our purposes is that both definitions include any group that provides health care services and participates in a formal peer-review process for the purpose of furthering quality healthcare.

---

[7] NPDB, "Reporting Medical Malpractice Payments," available at https://www.npdb.hrsa.gov/guidebook/EMMPR.jsp; HRSA, "NPDB Guidebook," October 2018, at E-27.
[8] *Id.* at E-18.
[9] *Id.* at E-19.
[10] 42 U.S.C. § 11151(6); 11151(8).
[11] *Id.* § 11151(4)(A).
[12] 45 CFR § 60.3.

"Health care services" is not defined (its meaning is probably well understood), but "formal peer-review process is the conduct of professional review activities through formally adopted written procedures which provide for adequate notice and an opportunity for a hearing."[13]

Setting the hospital section aside (because if you work for a hospital, you're likely already covered), let's put everything we've learned about the Corporate Shield together into one simple rule: A medical malpractice payment that would otherwise require a report to the NPDB is not reportable if the payment was made on behalf of a clinic or group practice that participates in a qualifying formal peer-review process.

Now we have our formula. If you're a medical practice owner, you'll want to (1) qualify as a group, and (2) participate in a qualifying formal peer-review process.

To qualify as a group, you'll need at least two "physicians" or "practitioners." That includes any two of the following: MD, DO, DDS, DMD, nurse practitioner, physician's assistant, registered nurse, dental hygienist, or *any other individual licensed or otherwise authorized by the state to provide health care services.*[14]

If you have at least that, you'll want to adopt a formal resolution within your business to establish yourselves as a clinical practice group or group practice. You'll want to get with a lawyer to prepare that correctly.

You'll also want to enroll in a qualifying formal peer-review process which requires, at a minimum, regular participation (at least annually).

That may sound onerous if you're trying to do it on your own, but you know what's even more onerous? Facing down a lawsuit knowing that if you settle, your name goes permanently on the blacklist for doctors.

Let's Talk Practicality: How Does It Work?

It's not enough to just have a qualifying clinical practice group. There are procedural requirements related to the lawsuit that we have to ensure are met.

---

[13] *Id.*; HRSA, "NPDB Guidebook," October 2018, at B-7.
[14] 42 U.S.C. 11151(6) & 11151(8).

The plaintiff/patient (and even their attorney) are not aware of the nuances of NPDB reporting. And why should they be? Plaintiff's attorneys don't represent doctors, and don't particularly care about them. For that matter, many defense attorneys only have a cursory understanding of the NPDB, if they know anything about it at all.

So when the plaintiff sues you, they're going to put your name on the lawsuit, even if you have set up a clinic or group practice and are participating in a qualifying peer-review program. What then? If it's a case you want to settle, your insurer would be making a payment on your behalf, not on behalf of your clinic, so they'll also be required to send a report to the NPDB.

For this to work, the clinic, not you individually, would have to be the defendant, and it would have to be on its behalf that the payment is made.

If it's not a case you want to settle, then none of this matters. You can take your case to trial, fight it, and all else being equal, you're more likely to win than the plaintiff.[15] That's still more of a risk than many doctors want to take. Even given the stiff consequences for settling, only 7% of medical malpractice cases go to trial.[16]

Settlement for doctors may usually come with a permanent NPDB black mark, but the only way you'll find yourself at the wrong end of a runaway jury is if you go to trial and lose.

The average malpractice jury verdict is around $800,000.[17] That's likely below your coverage limit.[18] But that's just an average. What happens if you go to trial and lose and you're on the high end of the range?

You can scour the internet if you like looking for high medical malpractice verdicts. They're scary, and they're everywhere. I don't

---

[15] According to one report, medical malpractice plaintiffs who go to trial win their case 21% of the time. Canady, MR. June 11, 2018, *Physician Leadership*, "The Verdict Is In: Surviving a Medical Malpractice Trial," available at https://www.physicianleaders.org/articles/the-verdict-surviving-medical-malpractice-trial, last accessed January 12, 2023. According to another report, even in cases with strong evidence of negligence, plaintiffs only win half the time, and in all other cases, the jury sides with the doctor 70–90% of the time. Peters, PG Jr. "Twenty Years of Evidence on the Outcomes of Malpractice Claims," *Clin. Orthop. Relat. Res.* Feb; 467(2): 352–57 (2009). Another report estimates that of all medical malpractice trials, plaintiffs win only 25%. U.S. Department of Justice, "Bureau of Justice Statistics Special Report" March 3, 2007, available at https://bjs.ojp.gov/content/pub/pdf/mmicss04.pdf, last accessed January 12, 2023.
[16] U.S. Department of Justice "Bureau of Justice Statistics Special Report" at 3.
[17] Canady, "The Verdict Is In," *Physician Leadership*.
[18] You more than likely have at least $1,000,000 in coverage.

have to go far to find examples of these. There are two attorneys I know personally in two different states who have either set the record for malpractice verdicts in their jurisdictions or came pretty close:

- Kent Buckingham won $73.2 million in a New Mexico medical malpractice case against Dr. Jerry McLaughlin and his employer Pecos Valley of New Mexico.[19]
- Jim Lyons won $46.5 million in an Arkansas medical malpractice case against Dr. Jonathan Lewis, and his employer Ouachita Valley Family Clinic.[20]

Those are scary numbers, so it's understandable that, if given the option, most doctors choose to settle. If it is a case you'd like to settle, you're going to need to get the plaintiff's cooperation to make sure your name doesn't go on the list.

In my experience litigating civil cases for over ten years, once real opportunity for settlement is on the table, much of the animosity and adversity that may have been present in the case is replaced by a spirit of cooperation—why wouldn't the plaintiff cooperate in efforts designed to put money in their pocket?

For this reporting exception to work, the plaintiff has to agree to dismiss you from the case completely, replacing you with the clinic or group practice. That requires a motion, and if it's jointly filed by both parties, the judge will likely just rubber-stamp it. But don't wait too long. Many local rules impose a deadline for amending the complaint to add new parties,[21] so be mindful of any applicable limits in your case.

There are some careful legal considerations to be made during this process to ensure you don't trigger the NPDB reporting. For example, dismissal from a lawsuit in exchange for payment is reportable: "A practitioner named, identified, or described in the written

---

[19] Stelnicki, T. August 25, 2018, *Santa Fe New Mexican*, "Santa Fe Jury Awards $73.2M in Delivery That Left Infant Disabled," available at: https://www.santafenewmexican.com/news/local_news/santa-fe-jury-awards-73-2m-in-delivery-that-left-infant-disabled/article_90275cd1-7a37-5b46-b232-20c0989668a5.html, last accessed November 9, 2023.

[20] Ratzan Law Group, PA, March 10, 2019, *Cision PR Newswire*, "Arkansas Jury Enters $46.5 Million Verdict for Toddler in Medical Malpractice Case," available at https://www.prnewswire.com/news-releases/arkansas-jury-enters-465-million-verdict-for-toddler-in-medical-malpractice-case-300422217.html, last accessed January 12, 2023.

[21] *E.g.*, NRCP 16.1(c)(2)(M).

complaint or claim who is subsequently dismissed from the lawsuit and not named, identified, or described in the settlement release should not be reported to the NPDB unless the dismissal results from a condition in the settlement or release."[22]

It's a delicate process, but if done correctly, you can have your cake and eat it too: you can settle a malpractice case without having your name reported to the NPDB.

Attempts to Eliminate the Corporate Shield

The Corporate Shield "loophole," whether intended or not, has since been embraced by the NPDB. It forms a part of the official narrative now. Although it was born more from what the statute doesn't say than what it does, the NPDB has leaned into it, and it is now part of the official NPDB Guidebook[23] and their website.[24]

At one point, though, way back in 1998, the HHS issued a notice of proposed rulemaking (NPRM) proposing to change the law to eliminate this reporting exception:

> It has come to the Department's attention that there have been instances in which a plaintiff in a malpractice action has agreed to dismiss a defendant health care practitioner from a proceeding, leaving or substituting a hospital or other corporate entity as defendant, at least in part for the purpose of allowing the practitioner to avoid having a report on a malpractice payment made on his or her behalf submitted to the Data Bank.[25]

The proposed new rule would have broadened the reporting requirement to require a report for "each practitioner whose acts or omissions were the basis of the action or claim,"[26] regardless of

---

[22] HRSA, "NPDB Guidebook," October 2018, at E-20.
[23] NPDB, "Reporting Medical Malpractice Payments," available at https://www.npdb.hrsa.gov/guidebook/EMMPR.jsp; HRSA, "NPDB Guidebook," October 2018, at E-19 and E-27.
[24] NPDB, "Reporting Medical Malpractice Payments," available at https://www.npdb.hrsa.gov/guidebook/EMMPR.jsp
[25] 63 FR 71255–57, "National Practitioner Data Bank for Adverse Information on Physicians and Other Health Care Practitioners: Medical Malpractice Payments Reporting Requirements," available at http://www.gpo.gov/fdsys/pkg/FR-1998-12-24/pdf/FR-1998-12-24.pdf, last accessed January 12, 2023.
[26] *Id.*

whether they were named in the complaint or a defendant at the time of settlement. This would require insurers to identify all practitioners, whether or not they were *ever a part of the lawsuit*.

In an update a year and a half later, the HHS reported, "Given the large number of thoughtful comments and the high level of concern that was voiced about the potential impact of the proposal as published, HRSA [Health Resources and Services Administration] believes it is imperative to gather additional data and conduct further analyses before proceeding."[27] They announced that they would issue a second notice of proposed rulemaking, anticipated by the end of 2000.[28]

That never happened. And over the next seven years, the HHS made no fewer than ten announcements, delaying the proposed new rule with no explanation, with subsequent announcements becoming more vague as to the anticipated action until it vanished altogether.[29]

Not everyone was happy with the HHS's unwillingness to broaden the reporting requirement to eliminate the corporate shield. One of those organizations, the Public Citizen Project, has made several efforts to close this loophole and end the Corporate Shield protections for medical practitioners.

In 2014, Public Citizen wrote a petition to the HHS and HRSA requesting that they amend the rules to close the corporate shield loophole.[30]

The HRSA issued a polite non-response that basically said "thank you for your thoughtful letter; rest assured that we regularly consider all options for improvement to NPDB reporting."[31]

---

[27] 65 FR 20428, "National Practitioner Data Bank for Adverse Information on Physicians and Other Health Care Practitioners: Medical Malpractice Payments Reporting Requirements," available at https://www.govinfo.gov/content/pkg/FR-2000-04-17/pdf/00-9470.pdf, last accessed January 12, 2023.
[28] *Id.*
[29] Teninbaum, GH. "Reforming the National Practitioner Data Bank to Promote Fair Med-Mal Outcomes," 5 *Wm. & Mary Pol'y Rev.* 83, 101 (2013).
[30] May 29, 2014 Letter from Public Citizen to the Department of Health and Human Services and Health Resources and Services Administration, available at https://www.citizen.org/wp-content/uploads/2203.pdf, last accessed August 24, 2023.
[31] June 16, 2014 Letter from HRSA to Public Citizen, available at https://www.citizen.org/wp-content/uploads/2203_June-16-2014-HRSA-initial-response-to-petition.pdf, last accessed August 24, 2023.

Two years later in July 2016, Public Citizen filed a lawsuit aiming to force the HHS to act on its 2014 petition.[32]

In response, the HRSA responded to the lawsuit with a less polite (even snarky) letter:

> Given the lack of a response from Public Citizen to HRSA's June 16, 2014 letter, HRSA believed that Public Citizen considered that letter a sufficient answer. HRSA now understands that Public Citizen apparently did not view that response as sufficient.
>
> HRSA has carefully reviewed your request and hereby denies Public Citizen's Petition for HRSA to engage in rulemaking to address the "corporate shield." As Public Citizen is aware, HRSA issued an NPRM on December 24, 1998 (63 FR 71255), to address the "corporate shield." HRSA received a large number of thoughtful comments regarding the proposed regulatory change, with the large majority of commenters voicing opposition. Among other concerns, commenters suggested that: (i) the method chosen in the NPRM was overbroad; (ii) the current regulations are adequate to address the problem; (iii) HHS may not have the legal authority to address this issue through regulation; (iv) the NPRM's assertion that the current regulations are inconsistent with the intent and purposes of the statute may not be accurate; and (v) addressing the "corporate shield" needs to be done in a manner that is both fair to practitioners and not burdensome for medical malpractice payers."

* * *

> In HRSA's view, the regulatory solution proposed in the NPRM and again suggested by Public Citizen in its May 2014 letter is not a viable answer for many of the reasons raised by commenters to the 1998 NPRM. Though HRSA remains open as to how to address the "corporate shield," HRSA is currently unaware of any regulatory mechanism that does not raise

---

[32] *Public Citizen, Inc. v. Department of Health and Human Services, et al.,* United States District Court for the District of Colombia, No. 16-1520, available at https://www.citizen.org/wp-content/uploads/public-citizen-v-hhs-complaint.pdf, last accessed August 24, 2023.

similar concerns. Accordingly, it denies Public Citizen's request to engage in rulemaking on that subject at this time.[33]

There is no guarantee that the corporate shield exception to the NPDB reporting requirement will not be eliminated or narrowed, but for now, it appears to be here to stay.[34]

---

[33] June 16, 2014, Letter from HRSA to Public Citizen, available at https://www.citizen.org/wp-content/uploads/2203_HRSA-Final-Response-Denying-Petition_Sept-212016.pdf, last accessed January 12, 2023.

[34] Given the amount of passion in its documented history, I am still surprised that some doctors have never heard of it, or tell me their defense attorney tells them there are no reporting requirements. "Why hasn't my attorney ever heard of it? He does nothing but medical malpractice defense." I am not sure how to respond to questions like this. Maybe ask your insurer to assign you a new attorney?

CHAPTER 5

Protecting Yourself from Your Patients (While Protecting Them, Too!)

We have discussed at length the measures medical practitioners can take to arm themselves in the case of a lawsuit. To make it possible to move forward, settle if desired, and avoid having your name reported.

Nothing in life, or the law, is guaranteed, of course, but there is a lot you can do to protect yourself if you do find yourself in the uncomfortable position where you are facing a claim or action.

However, one method we haven't talked about for keeping your name off that list is taking precautionary measures to prevent the lawsuit or claim from ever happening. It's one thing to take medication to manage or treat the symptoms of a disease. It's something else altogether to maintain a lifestyle where those preventable diseases are never contracted.

I have chosen to call this approach "legal prophylaxis," for reasons that should be very obvious to your medically trained mind.

This prophylactic approach requires us to look at the reasons practitioners have claims brought against them and then do what we can to mitigate that risk.

For a complete picture, let's identify who is suing doctors, then we'll examine why (it's not always as obvious as you'd think).

There is one question that will help us in this analysis more than any other: with whom do doctors have relationships in their capacity as medical professionals? The answer is simple: the most common relationships are those with patients and employees.

In this chapter, let's scrutinize why doctors are having claims brought against them by their patients and then discover what we can do to minimize the ensuing lawsuits. In the following chapter, we'll review claims relating to employees.

Why Patients Sue Doctors

If you ask a doctor why they've been sued by their patients, their answers almost always relate to medical care and outcomes. In a medical survey of 4,000 physicians about why they were sued, the top responses were as follows:[1]

- Failure to diagnose: 31%
- Patient suffered an abnormal injury: 31%
- Failure to treat: 12%
- Poor documentation of patient instruction and education: 4%
- Errors in medical administration: 4%
- Failure to follow safety procedures: 3%
- Improperly obtaining/lack of informed consent: 3%

These answers are probably informed by the allegations made in the complaint, where the plaintiff is required to allege enough to put the doctor on notice of the accusations against them.[2]

If these were the real reasons for a lawsuit, you would expect far more lawsuits to be filed. Doctor makes a harmful mistake, doctor gets sued. You would expect a high correlation between the degree of harm and incidence of lawsuits—the worse the mistake, the more likely the lawsuit.

But the numbers don't support that conclusion. Let's look at the number of medical-error-related deaths and compare it to the number of lawsuits to get an idea how much the results alone drive the decision to sue.

Numerous sources have attempted to quantify the number of deaths resulting from medical error, though such an effort is

---

[1] Peckham, C. "Medscape Malpractice Report 2015: Why Most Doctors Get Sued," December 9, 2015, available at https://www.medscape.com/features/slideshow/public/malpractice-report-2015, last accessed November 2, 2023.

[2] *See, e.g.,* Fed. R. Civ. P. 8.

problematic. For one thing, "medical error," which is nothing more than departing from the elusive standard of care (which standard of care is always changing with medical advances), is something that normally takes multiple lawyers, expert witnesses, tens of thousands of dollars, and an empaneled jury to decide, so an ad hoc review of some medical records can't by any means be a definitive determination. Moreover, the medical professionals charting the patient's progress have a strong disincentive not to provide incriminating information in their documentation. And finally, Centers for Disease Control does not recognize "medical error" as officially recognized cause of death, so in every case where a patient dies, there is some medical reason for it that may or may not have anything to do with the treatment or the physician.

Notwithstanding these limitations, efforts have been made to perform a quantitative analysis, and the results, unsurprisingly, have a large range. The Institute of Medicine estimated the annual death toll resulting from medical error at 98,000.[3] Dr. Sonjay Gupta's published estimate was 200,000.[4] Johns Hopkins places that number at 250,000.[5] Other medical journals have that number as high as 440,000,[6] which would account for one out of every six deaths in this country.

That's a large range, but it's what we have to work with.

The NPDB reported receiving 3,046 reports for payments resulting from a wrongful death claim or action in a single year.[7] Those would not include non-reportable settlements, cases where the reporting entity failed to provide the report, or cases where the doctor prevailed.

Recognizing that the numbers we do have aren't perfect, we can nonetheless estimate the prevalence of claims resulting from wrongful death.

---

[3] Kohn LT, Corrigan JM, Donaldson MS, editors. *To Err Is Human: Building a Safer Health System.* Washington, DC: National Academies Press (2000). This estimate was based on data from patients treated in New York hospitals in 1984.
[4] Gupta, S. July 31, 2012, *New York Times,* "More Treatment, More Mistakes."
[5] Johns Hopkins Medicine, "Study Suggests Medical Errors Now Third Leading Cause of Death in the U.S.," May 3, 2016.
[6] James, JT. "A New, Evidence-based Estimate of Patient Harms Associated with Hospital Care," 9 (3) *Journal of Patient Safety* 122–28 (2013).
[7] That year was 2013. Gottlieb, E. & Doroshow, J. "Medical Malpractice: By the Numbers," December *Ctr. for Just. & Democracy* 2 (2015).

We know that only 7% of malpractice cases go to trial,[8] and of those, physicians win roughly 80% of the time.[9] If those numbers hold true for wrongful death cases, then in addition to the 3,046 wrongful death cases that resulted in a loss or settlement by the doctor, there would be another 181 wrongful death cases where the doctor went to trial and won.[10] That's a total of 3,227 wrongful death cases.

If death by cause of medical negligence happens between 80,000 and 440,000 times per year, then lawsuits are only brought for between 0.73% and 4.03% of all wrongful deaths.

So how can we account for the fact that for every person who sues for wrongful death, there are between 25 and 100 people who have also suffered death of a loved one due to medical negligence but who do not bring a claim? Whatever the reason, it has to be more than just the outcome.

If you ask the plaintiffs why they sued, a different pattern emerges than when you ask the doctor. They don't speak in medical or legal terms. Plaintiffs speak in more human terms:[11]

- They were injured
- They experienced insensitive handling and poor communication after the incident
- They felt that when a doctor provided an explanation, more than 85% of explanations were unsatisfactory

When asked what they wanted from the lawsuit, they were even more specific:[12]

- Concern for standards of care (preventing similar incidents in the future)

---

[8] U.S. Department of Justice "Bureau of Justice Statistics Special Report" at 3.
[9] Canady, "The Verdict Is In," *Physician Leadership*.
[10] If 3,406 make up the 94.4% of cases where the doctor did not go to trial and win (7% of all cases go to trial, and of those, doctors win 80%, which means of all cases, doctors go to trial and win 80% x 7% = 5.6% of the time, leaving 94.4% where the doctors do not go to trial and win.) These numbers also suggest doctors settle too quickly. If doctors win roughly 80% of the trials, but they are only going to trial 7% of the time, that means they are settling 93% of the time even though if they went to trial, they'd have an 80% chance of winning. Add to that if more doctors took the case all the way to trial, fewer attorneys would be willing to take malpractice cases.
[11] Vincent, C, Young, M, & Phillips, A. "Why Do People Sue Doctors? A Study of Patients and Relatives Taking Legal Action." 343(8913) *Lancet*, 1609–13 (1994). available at https://doi.org/10.1016/s0140-6736(94)93062-7, last accessed January 12, 2023.
[12] *Id.*

- Explanation (how did it happen and why?)
- Compensation for losses
- Accountability

Put another way, two of the three reasons given for suing have nothing to do with the injury, and two of the four things they want out of a lawsuit are things a lawsuit cannot directly provide!

For ten years I was a trial attorney, and for much of that, I represented plaintiffs who sued doctors. My personal experience jibes with what we're seeing here. Most people who are wronged by doctors (or have the perception that they were), do not want to sue. There is usually an injury, yes, but they sought answers, explanations, and reassurances from the doctor, and were given curt explanations, stonewalled, or dismissed as a patient. The doctor would no longer speak to them, and they didn't know where else to turn.

The doctor was the villain, not because of the negative outcome, but because of how the matter was handled after the negative outcome!

I honestly believe that most lawsuits can be avoided, irrespective of the injury, if the doctor is willing to put the worry of litigation aside, drop the physician's pride, and be a compassionate human being with someone who is confused, hurting, and ofttimes alone.[13]

If you're like most doctors (81% by one report),[14] you don't agree with me. You think an apology would do no good. In some cases, that's probably true. And although an apology is only one piece of the equation, let's look at this a little closer.

Don't Avoid the Patient When Something Goes Wrong; Consider Apologizing

Conventional wisdom in healthcare is that if something goes wrong, the doctor should avoid the patient—avoid the risk of saying something that could implicate yourself in a future lawsuit.

---

[13] Hold the presses! I'm a lawyer suggesting people prevent lawsuits? How will I pay for my kids' education?

[14] Meklir, SA, Schwartz, S. "Why Doctors Are Sued Most Often ... And Why?", available at https://www.sommerspc.com/blog/2016/04/which-doctors-are-sued-most-often, last accessed January 12, 2023.

The American Medical Association's first Code of Ethics, published in 1847, recommended physicians closely monitor their words and behavior, and "avoid all things which have a tendency to discourage the patient and to depress his spirits." A popular physician training manual written around the turn of the 20th century recommended that physicians be "at liberty to be silent or to say but little regarding the nature or degree of a person's sickness ... in every stage of your career aim to convince the world that you, as a physician, are an apostle of hope ... and that your profession is not in league with the grim forces of death and mourning, but that, on the contrary, all its characteristics are indicative of health-giving and life-restoring power" For many years, physicians were encouraged to instill optimism in patients, at the expense of full disclosure.[15]

The problem with this "wisdom" is that the avoidance is often just as frustrating as the medical outcome. Patients are left feeling confused, abandoned, and betrayed. How a doctor deals with the problem can be as predicable a factor in whether litigation will occur as the outcome of the procedure or treatment. "Physicians who appear to be insensitive, unavailable, or critical are much more likely to be sued."[16] In many cases, an apology with an explanation can be enough to prevent what otherwise would have been a lawsuit.

"Apologies—statements that acknowledge an error and its consequences, take responsibility, and communicate regret for having caused harm—can decrease blame, decrease anger, increase trust, and improve relationships."[17]

In a survey of patients-turned-plaintiffs, about 40% reported that if they had received an explanation and apology, they would never have felt like they needed to sue.[18] Study after study confirms that the choice to sue is related to the doctor's poor communication and unwillingness to be forthcoming about what went wrong.[19]

---

[15] Ross, NE & Newman, WJ. "The Role of Apology Laws in Medical Malpractice," May *Journal of the American Academy of Psychiatry and the Law* (2021) https://jaapl.org/content/early/2021/05/19/JAAPL.200107-20.
[16] *Id.*
[17] Robbennolt JK. "Apologies and Medical Error," 467(2) *Clinical Orthopaedics and Related Research*, 376. (2009). https://doi.org/10.1007/s11999-008-0580-1.
[18] Vincent CA, Young M, Phillips A. "Why Do People Sue Doctors? A Study of Patients and Relatives Taking Legal Action," 343 *Lancet.* 1609–13 (1994).
[19] Beckman HB, Markakis KM, Suchman AL, Frankel RM. "The Doctor-Patient

Many hospitals that have introduced error disclosure programs have seen improvement in the area of medical malpractice. For example, the University of Michigan created a disclosure program in 2001, and after six years of data collection, they saw a 36% reduction in malpractice claims.[20] When a lawsuit did occur, it did not last as long, and its overall cost was reduced by 44%.[21] An academic health system in Tennessee reported similar improvements after implementing a disclosure program.[22]

The apology must be sincere, though. A bad apology is often worse than no apology at all:

> An effective apology generally contains four elements: the acknowledgment of harm, evidence of remorse, an offer to repair any damages, and the promise of behavioral change. Above all, an apology must be sincere. Many aspects of an apology signal sincerity, such as appropriate timing, a lack of defensiveness, clear evidence of reparative action, and an absence of any evident ulterior motives for apologizing (e.g., financial reward or avoidance of punishment).[23]

Relationship and Malpractice: Lessons From Plaintiff Depositions," 154 *Arch Intern Med* 1365–70 (1994); Hickson GB, Clayton EW, Githens PB, Sloan FA. "Factors That Prompted Families to File Medical Malpractice Claims Following Perinatal Injuries." 267 *JAMA* 1359–63 (1992); Hickson GB, Federspiel CF, Pichert JW, Miller CS, Gauld-Jaeger J, Bost P. "Patient Complaints and Malpractice Risk," 287 *JAMA* 2951–57 (2002); Huycke LI, Huycke MM. "Characteristics of Potential Plaintiffs in Malpractice Litigation," 120 *Ann Intern Med.* 792–98 (1994); Lester GW, Smith SG. "Listening and Talking to Patients: A Remedy for Malpractice Suits?" 158 *West J Med.* 268–72 (1993); Levinson W, Roter DL, Mullooly JP, Dull VT, Frankel RM. "Physician-Patient Communication: The Relationship With Malpractice Claims Among Primary Care Physicians And Surgeons," 177 *JAMA*177 553–59 (1997); Shapiro RS, Simpson DE, Lawrence SL, Talsky AM, Sobocinski KA, Schiedermayer DL. "A Survey of Sued and Nonsued Physicians and Suing Patients," 149 *Arch Intern Med.* 2190–96 (1989).

[20] Kachalia et al. "Liability Claims and Costs Before and After Implementation of a Medical Error Disclosure Program," 153 *Ann Intern Med*, 213–21 (2010).

[21] *Id.*

[22] LeCraw et al., "Changes in Liability Claims, Costs, and Resolution Times Following the Introduction of a Communication-and-Resolution Program in Tennessee," 23 *J Patient Saf Risk Manag.* 13–18, (2018).

[23] Ross & Newman, "The Role of Apology Laws in Medical Malpractice," citing Bolstad M., "Learning from Japan: The Case for Increased Use of Apology in Mediation," 48 *Clev St L Rev* 545–78, (2000); Daicoff S., "Apology, Forgiveness, Reconciliation & Therapeutic Jurisprudence," 13 *Pepp Disp Resol Law J*, 131–80 (2013); O'Hara EA et al. "On Apology and Consilience," 77 *Wash L Rev* 1121–92 (2002).

Most doctors want to explain; they want to apologize.[24] But in practice, few do.[25] There are many reasons for this, some of them probably sound.

But as a medical professional, when something goes wrong (and something will), evidence suggests that you should at least consider apologizing. It can improve patient relations, prevent a lawsuit (or encourage settlement at a lower cost), and undoubtedly reduce any guilt the medical professional may feel.

Practice Medicine, Not Defensive Medicine

You have probably heard the term "defensive medicine." It isn't a medical term. It is a legal one. Congress defined defensive medicine as occurring "when doctors order tests, procedures, or visits, or avoid certain high-risk patients or procedures, primarily (but not necessarily) because of concern about malpractice liability."[26]

The practice of defensive medicine has been blamed for being partially responsible for the U.S.'s overly high healthcare costs, with some estimates placing the costs associated with defensive medicine at $45 billion annually.[27] The 1,020 hospitalists surveyed nationally estimated that almost 40% of healthcare-related resources in their practices were a direct result of defensive medicine.[28] Orthopedic surgeons estimated that 24% of their tests were medically unnecessary.[29] An estimated 73% to 92% of private sector physicians order unnecessary tests for their own protection.[30]

Although it is true that the medical professional has a financial incentive to order more tests (they get to charge for administering

---

[24] Kaldjian, LC et al., "Disclosing Medical Errors to Patients: Attitudes and Practices of Physicians and Trainees," 22 *J Gen Intern Med*, 988–96, (2007).
[25] *Id.*
[26] U.S. Congress, Office of Technology Assessment. "Defensive Medicine and Medical Malpractice." Washington, DC: U.S. Government Printing Office OTA-H-602, July 1994.
[27] Mello MM, Chandra A, Gawande AA, Studdert DM. "National Costs of the Medical Liability System," 29 *Health Aff* 1569–77 (2010).
[28] Saint, S., et al. "Perception of Resources Spent on Defensive Medicine and History of Being Sued Among Hospitalists: Results from a National Survey," January *Journal of Hospital Medicine* (2018).
[29] Gupta, S. July 31, 2012, *New York Times* "More Treatment, More Mistakes," available at https://www.nytimes.com/2012/08/01/opinion/more-treatment-more-mistakes.html, last accessed November 2, 2023.
[30] Sonal Sekhar, M. et al. "Defensive Medicine: A Bane to Healthcare," Apr-Jun *Annals of Medical & Health Sciences Research* (2013).

and interpreting those tests, after all), there is something far more relevant to the doctor than the costs of healthcare: the practice of defensive medicine actually increases the probability of doing harm. Defensive medicine is meant to protect the doctor, not the patient, though inevitably when a doctor changes their focus away from the patient, it becomes more difficult to "do no harm," and the doctor is neither protecting themselves nor the patient.

> Herein lies a stunning irony. Defensive medicine is rooted in the goal of avoiding mistakes. But each additional procedure or test, no matter how cautiously performed, injects a fresh possibility of error. CT and M.R.I. scans can lead to false positives and unnecessary operations, which carry the risk of complications like infections and bleeding. The more medications patients are prescribed, the more likely they are to accidentally overdose or suffer an allergic reaction. Even routine operations like gallbladder removals require anesthesia, which can increase the risk of heart attack and stroke.[31]

One publication described defensive medicine as an "epidemic":

> Defensive medicine has been practiced for decades and spread to countries the world over to become an epidemic, causing unnecessary hospitalizations, tests, invasive procedures, drug prescriptions, consultations with other physicians, avoidance of high risk patients, and congested waiting lists. This can cause serious consequences. For example, in a patient with an infection a physician practicing defensive medicine may prolong antibiotic duration, prescribe unnecessary broad-spectrum antibiotics or combinations of agents, or prescribe unnecessary antibiotic treatments, which may contribute to the alarming spread of antibiotic resistance. Even students and residents frequently encounter defensive medicine practices and are in various instances taught to take malpractice liability into consideration when making clinical decisions. Medicolegal systems tend to censure alleged errors of omission much more often than any other type of fault, thus incentivizing a

---

[31] Gupta, S. July 31, 2012, *New York Times* "More Treatment, More Mistakes."

continuously increasing and excessive number of diagnostic investigations as a strategy for reducing legal risk.[32]

Defensive medicine, by its very definition, is a violation of the Hippocratic Oath: "I will prescribe regimen for the good of my patients according to my ability and my judgment and never do harm to anyone."

Medicine should be practiced based on the needs of the patient, not the needs of the doctor. And when the doctor focuses on the patient, and not themselves, there are fewer mistakes, and less litigation.

Use a Checklist

Little works better for ensuring routine exercises are done correctly than using a checklist. Pilots go through a pre-flight checklist before every take-off. Retail managers use checklists for opening stores. Escape room game masters use checklists to reset the rooms for the next players. Anyone using a recipe is just following a checklist.

In any situation where there are simple routines that have to be repeated over and over again, a checklist is helpful to make sure it is done correctly. A dentist may require their assistant to use a checklist when setting up the tray to ensure all the tools are there when the dentist is working on the patient. A nurse may use a checklist when performing a physical to make sure every vital is taken and recorded.

The higher the stakes, the more important it is not to miss something small. In a comprehensive two-year study in eight cities across the world in various socioeconomic strata, checklists came across as a clear lifesaver. The rate of major complications in surgery fell by 36%. Deaths decreased by 47%. Post-op return visits by patients due to bleeding or other technical problems fell by 25%.[33]

But checklists don't just improve success rates. They also improve morale and teamwork. A Johns Hopkins study measured the use of a checklist's effect on teamwork. Eleven surgeons used checklists in their cases for three months, after which 92% of the team members involved reported that they "functioned as a well-coordinated team," up from 68% prior to the use of the checklist.[34]

---

[32] Vento, S. et al., "Defensive Medicine: It Is Time to Finally Slow Down an Epidemic," October *World Journal of Clinical Cases* (2018).
[33] Gawande, A. *The Checklist Manifesto*. London, England: Profile Books (2011) at 153.
[34] *Id* at 108.

At the Kaiser hospitals, use of a checklist for six months in 3,500 operations had a profound impact on morale. Reported employee satisfaction rose by 19%, and nurse turnover decreased from 23% to 7%.[35]

Despite these staggering numbers, many doctors, and surgeons in particular, have resisted the use of checklists in their practice.[36]

Don't be too proud to use something as simple as a checklist. It could dramatically improve your patients' prognosis, and as a byproduct, substantially reduce the likelihood that a patient wants to hold you to account.

How to Properly Terminate a Patient

As hard as it is to find and keep new patients, sometimes there is a patient we no longer want to treat. We want to terminate the provider-patient relationship.

If you owned a restaurant, or an auto body shop, as long as you aren't discriminating against a protected class, in most cases you wouldn't have to do anything more than notify the client you are no longer going to do business with them, and that would be enough.

As a medical professional, though, it may not be that easy.

Once the provider-patient relationship is created, you have a heightened duty of care to the patient. The patient has placed their health and well-being, sometimes their lives, in your hands, and you have accepted that responsibility.

This duty could come from a contractual promise, it could come from statute, or it could be implied from the circumstances. Regardless of its source, breaching that duty could result in liability for malpractice, other negligence, or even patient abandonment.

To protect yourself in these situations, you're going to want to adopt a three-part strategy: (1) only create provider-patient relationships that you intend to create, (2) fulfill your duties to your current patients, and (3) establish and follow clear protocols for terminating patient relationships (which discharges the duty of care).

Our focus in the next section is on stage one. The second stage is more medical than legal and is undoubtedly covered extensively in those continuing education courses you attend every year, so we

---

[35] *Id.*
[36] *Id.* at 155–56.

won't cover that any further. The chapter concludes with stage three, providing you with information on ending patient relationships.

Only Create Provider-Patient Relationships That You Intend to Create

In most cases, the provider-patient relationship is established when the patient walks into your office and fills out the new-patient paperwork. In those cases, you control the narrative. The terms of the relationship, the expectations of both parties, and several other relationship-defining promises are made clear in black and white on a document the patient signs.

But sometimes that provider-patient relationship is created much more subtly. Case law on this subject is by no means universal or consistent:

- A medical provider who stopped to aid a stranger in immediate need of medical care created a provider-patient relationship "and thereby assumed a duty of reasonable care towards the patient."[37]
- A doctor who accepted another doctor's referral established a provider-patient relationship with the referred patient.[38]
- A doctor who made medical decisions about treatment rendered by other doctors created a provider-patient relationship with patient,[39] even when he just discussed case over the phone with another physician and gave advice as to how patient should be treated.[40]
- A doctor who provided a 90-minute consultation with patient established provider-patient relationship.[41]
- A "doctor who evaluated medical information about a patient and made a medical decision about whether to transfer her to another hospital" established provider-patient relationship.[42]

---

[37] *Colby v. Schwartz*, 78 Cal. App. 3d 885, 890, 144 Cal. Rptr. 624, 627 (Ct. App. 1978).
[38] *Bovara v. St. Francis Hosp.*, 298 Ill.App.3d 1025, 233 Ill.Dec. 42, 700 N.E.2d 143, 146 (Ill.App.Ct.1998).
[39] *DeLong v. Nelson*, No. CV 17-11783-PBS, 2019 WL 4193423, at *12 (D. Mass. Sept. 3, 2019).
[40] *Pope v. St. John*, 862 S.W.2d 657 (Tex.App.—Austin 1993).
[41] *White v. Harris*, 2011 VT 115, ¶ 9, 190 Vt. 647, 650, 36 A.3d 203, 206 (2011).
[42] *Wheeler v. Yettie Kersting Memorial Hosp.*, 866 S.W.2d 32 (Tex.App.—Houston [1st Dist.] (1993).

- A doctor who examined a patient at their employer's request and solely for employer's benefit did not create a provider-patient relationship unless doctor were to have injured patient by providing affirmative treatment or advice related to a course of treatment.[43]
- A doctor who took "some action to treat the patient" where no prior relationship existed established a provider-patient relationship. An agreement to be on-call did not in and of itself establish such a relationship.[44]
- A medical provider who agreed to go to hospital in response to specific patient's needs, did not alone, without more, establish the provider-patient relationship.[45]
- A doctor who makes a statement that he would examine patient did not establish provider-patient relationship.[46]
- A physician who examined an X-ray of patient as a favor to a member of the hospital staff without ever speaking to patient or patient's family did not establish a provider-patient relationship.[47]
- A doctor who "Mere[ly] examin[ed] an individual, in the absence of an agreement to benefit the patient, [did] not constitute acceptance of that individual as a patient."[48]
- A medical provider who made a public mission statement to provide "quantitative assessment and disposition for individuals in the Boston Area who require emergency psychiatric services" did not do enough to create provider-patient relationship with all individuals in the Boston Area or even those who encountered the program.[49]

There are hundreds of other cases where one of the court's central issues was determining whether the provider-patient relationship was formed, and invariably, the doctor insisted that it had not been, but the patient insisted that it had. Notably, none of the cases I read

---

[43] *Heller v. Peekskill Cmty. Hosp.*, 198 A.D.2d 265, 265–66, 603 N.Y.S.2d 548, 549–50 (1993).
[44] *Day v. Harkins & Munoz*, 961 S.W.2d 278, 280–81 (Tex. App. 1997).
[45] *Ortiz v. Shah*, 905 S.W.2d 609, 611 (Tex. App. 1995), writ denied (Nov. 16, 1995).
[46] *Roberts v. Hunter*, 310 S.C. 364, 426 S.E.2d 797 (S.C.1993).
[47] *Minster v. Pohl*, 206 Ga. App. 617, 619, 426 S.E.2d 204, 206 (1992).
[48] *Hord v. United States*, 178 F.3d 1283 (4th Cir. 1999) (citing *Tumblin v. Ball-Incon Glass Packaging Corp.*, 324 S.C. 359, 478 S.E.2d 81, 85 (S.C.Ct.App.1996)).
[49] *Garcia v. City of Bos.*, 115 F. Supp. 2d 74, 78 (D. Mass. 2000), aff'd, 253 F.3d 147 (1st Cir. 2001).

involved a written contract—it's always the cases on the margins that get litigated.

The lesson here is to be careful and deliberate when it comes to discussing someone's health with them. Be mindful that your intentions are clear, especially in the following situations where the putative patient is not coming into your office:

- Phone calls and emails
- Telemedicine
- Social media interactions
- Other medical professionals seeking your advice
- Favor for family or friend
- Independent Medical Exams, employer physicals, and other examinations at the request of someone other than the person to be examined

Although it may be awkward to decline to offer free advice to a family member or friend, the safest route is going to be to refer them to another practitioner, decline to get involved unless they come into your office, or just fall back on the tried-and-true "liability" excuse (this is a discussion about liability, after all): "I would love to get involved here, but I'd be taking an undue risk and doing you a disservice if I offered advice without having collected your history, taken your vitals, and examined you. It's those dang lawyers. You know how it is. Liability at every corner."[50]

Establish and Follow Clear Protocols for Terminating Patient Relationships

Like the restaurant owner who posts a sign that says "we reserve the right to refuse service to anyone," you, too, have a right to decline to accept someone as a patient, or if they're already a patient, you can terminate the relationship.[51]

However, unlike the restaurant owner, you have far more to consider before ejecting a client from your place of business.

Some of those things you need to consider include the following:

- Emergency Care (e.g., EMTALA[52])

---

[50] When in doubt, blame attorneys!
[51] *See, e.g.,* Idaho Code 39-1391(c).
[52] Emergency Medical Treatment & Labor Act, 42 U.S.C. § 1395dd.

- Anti-discrimination laws[53]
- Contractual obligations[54]
- Charity care obligations
- Grant requirements
- Patient abandonment
- Local ethical requirements

Sometimes the application of these exceptions is easy. For example, if refusal to render medical care would violate your Hippocratic Oath and cause the patient harm, it's safe to say you have a duty to provide care. If you are refusing to accept a patient or are terminating a patient relationship because of prejudices you hold toward a specific protected class, that's a big no-no, too.

Although not an exhaustive list, there are also precedent-setting examples of when a doctor may lawfully dismiss a patient:

- Repeated noncompliance with treatment and follow up appointments that were previously agreed upon
- Disruptive, threatening, or seductive behavior
- Unreasonable failure to pay for services
- A physician's closure of their practice or retirement
- Misleading statements about the patient's past medical history
- Patient's chronic drug-seeking behaviors
- Criminal behavior at the office[55]

Although there are clear-cut examples on both sides, usually it's going to require examining the facts on a case-by-case basis, and the outcome will depend heavily on what happened in your situation.

If you are considering terminating a patient, you'll want to consider the following:

- What are the patient's current health needs? (If there is emergent care required, you are taking a bigger risk and

---

[53] *E.g.*, Title II of the Civil Rights Act, 42 U.S.C. § 2000(a). This provision applies to that restaurant owner, too.

[54] You may have a contract that requires you to continue care in certain situations.

[55] Jung S, McDowell RH. *Abandonment*. Treasure Island (FL): StatPearls Publishing; (2022), available at https://www.ncbi.nlm.nih.gov/books/NBK563285/, last accessed January 18, 2023.

subjecting the patient to more risk by terminating the relationship without safeguards in place.)

- How easy or difficult would it be for a patient to find necessary healthcare elsewhere within the time needed? (If you are the only provider in your field, and the patient needs care specific to your expertise, the more I'd think about it before dismissing the patient.)

- Is the patient in a protected class? (If they are, you'll want to examine not only your motives, but also your ability to prove your motives before terminating the relationship.)

As part of this analysis, you should look at what constitutes patient abandonment. One court summarized patient abandonment as follows:

When a physician takes charge of a case and is employed to attend a patient, the relation of physician and patient continues until ended by the mutual consent of the parties, or revoked by dismissal of the physician, or the physician determines that his services are no longer beneficial to the patient and then only upon giving to the patient a reasonable time in which to procure other medical attendance.[56]

Another court outlined three things a patient must prove to win a case for medical abandonment: (1) the unilateral severance of the doctor-patient relationship by the doctor; (2) without reasonable notice or without providing adequate alternative medical care; and (3) at a time when there is the necessity of continuing medical attention.[57] The standard for abandonment in your state may differ.

Only continue with the termination if you are convinced (consult an attorney if needed) that you can terminate the relationship in a way that will not be considered patient abandonment.

If at this point, you are still committed to terminating the relationship, consider your obligations to the patient as set forth by

---

[56] *Tierney v. Univ. of Michigan Regents*, 257 Mich. App. 681, 686, 669 N.W.2d 575, 578 (2003).
[57] *King v. Fisher*, 918 S.W.2d 108, 112 (Tex. App. 1996), writ denied (Oct. 10, 1996).

the AMA Principles of Medical Ethics (or the equivalent ADA Principles of Ethics for dentists)[58]:

> Physicians' fiduciary responsibility to patients entails an obligation to support continuity of care for their patients. At the beginning of patient-physician relationship, the physician should alert the patient to any foreseeable impediments to continuity of care.
>
> When considering withdrawing from a case, physicians must:
>
> (a) Notify the patient (or authorized decision maker) long enough in advance to permit the patient to secure another physician.
>
> (b) Facilitate transfer of care when appropriate.[59]

I would also recommend, before terminating the relationship, that you call your local ethics hotline and run the situation by them. They should have some good advice related to your local ethical rules. If nothing else, you will have shown that you were thoughtful in your termination, not only by re-reading through this section of the book,[60] but also by consulting with the ethics chapter of your local board.

Once you're committed to terminating the relationship, you're going to want to make sure you document everything. Send a written letter to the patient. The letter should provide a brief, valid reason for terminating the relationship, an agreement to continue to provide emergency treatment for a reasonable length of time (usually 30 days will be enough), during which time the patient can find a new provider. You may also consider offering to find a new provider for the patient and notifying the patient that you are happy to facilitate the transfer of records to the new provider.

It probably goes without saying but keep the language professional. Refrain from calling names or blaming the patient. This letter should serve to help you if the patient ever initiates a claim or lawsuit, not incriminate you or make you look like the bad guy.

---

[58] *See, e.g.,* ADA "Patient Dismissal," available at: https://www.ada.org/en/resources/practice/practice-management/managing-patients-dismissal, last accessed November 2, 2023.
[59] AMA Principles of Medical Ethics: I, VI.
[60] Feel free to disclose that if a patient makes an allegation that you improperly abandoned them—I can't guarantee it will help, but it can't hurt.

If there was a specific occurrence or occurrences that precipitated the termination, get witnesses to provide and sign objective statements. Objective the same way the medical charting would be. Instead of saying "the patient behaved in an aggressive and inappropriate way," document that "the patient raised her fists and her voice, leaned in towards Nurse Charlie, and said 'don't you dare get that popsicle stick anywhere near my mouth.'"

Everything you document should be put in the patient's chart.

Terminating patients can be tricky, but there is a right way and a wrong way to do it. Done right, you can minimize the risk of creating a claim, or if one is filed, you give yourself the best chance of defeating it.

CHAPTER 6

Protect Yourself from Your Employees (and from the Actions of Your Employees)

If you own a medical practice with employees, you need to consider not only your own interactions with patients but also those of your staff. Hang on, but it wasn't you who failed to record important information—in fact you weren't even in the room! That might not matter: there are two ways you can be held accountable for actions related to those you hire. First, you can be held directly liable for your failure to perform your role as an employer and supervisor. You have a legal duty to properly hire, train, and where necessary, fire your employees. A violation of this duty can result in liability for a tort called negligent hiring, training, and retention.[1]

Second, you can be held indirectly liable through a legal doctrine called *respondeat superior*, which is a form of vicarious liability that applies specifically to the employer/employee relationship. Vicarious liability makes it so one person can be completely legally responsible for the actions of another.[2] In the employer/employee relationship, it is well established that the employer is held responsible for the harmful actions of its employees undertaken within the scope of employment.[3] This liability has nothing to do with your own actions

---

[1] Different jurisdictions will have different names for this tort.
[2] *Am. Home Assur. Co. v. Nat'l R.R. Passenger Corp.*, 908 So. 2d 459, 467 (Fla. 2005).
[3] *Presbyterian Camp & Conf. Centers, Inc. v. Superior Ct.*, 12 Cal. 5th 493, 502, 501 P.3d 211, 217 (2021).

and is entirely based on the actions of the employees and their relationship to you. So if your nurse fails to follow the proper hygiene protocol with disastrous results, you could be responsible for that mistake even if you had trained, trained, and retrained to make sure that mistake never happened.

There are strategies you can adopt in both cases to minimize your risk of liability. The good news is, in most cases, the action required on your part is the same: make sure your hiring process, training, and employee retention practices are robust and legally sound and you'll reduce the chances of both direct and vicarious liability.

Proper Hiring

The first step in protecting yourself from the actions of your employees is to make sure you've got the right employees.

I'll leave it up to you to figure out if they're a good fit for the schedule you need, will interact with patients cheerily, etc. That's all important, but proper hiring in this context means you're not hiring a liability bomb waiting to go off.

You don't want to be the health center that hires Dr. Death[4] or the trucking company that hires drivers with a history of driving under the influence.[5]

Wait—why would a doctor care about trucking companies? If you are going to hire someone who will make deliveries or home visits for your practice, verify that their driver's license is current, check their criminal history, and get their driving history.

Hiring a nurse, hygienist, or physician? Make sure their license is current and they are CE compliant. If you have access, ping the NPDB to see what's there. Much of what is on the NPDB should be no cause for concern (see the rest of Part I), and if you see cause for concern, give the practitioner an opportunity to explain, but by making the query, you can show that you did due diligence in hiring. Put any results of the query, along with the practitioner's response, in their personnel file.

---

[4] Elbein, S. "'Dr. Death' Condemns Christopher Duntsch, but the Real Culprit Is Texas's Broken Healthcare System," *Texas Monthly*, July 15, 2021, available at https://www.texasmonthly.com/arts-entertainment/dr-death-christopher-duntsch-tv-series-review/, last accessed January 25, 2023.

[5] Trucking Truth, "Trucking Companies That Hire Drivers with DUI," available at https://www.truckingtruth.com/wiki/topic-55/trucking-company-policies-on-drivers-with-dui-dwi#less5, last accessed January 25, 2023.

Check social media. What kinds of posts do the physicians you want to employ make?

You know those references that the candidate for employment provides that you ignore? Give them a call or drop them an email.

The more you can do to show care in hiring, the more you'll be able to distinguish the good employees from the bad. And the better you will be able to prove that you were not negligent in your hiring.

Proper Training

Now that you have your staff hired, you will want to make sure they understand not just the responsibilities related to their position but also the bounds of the law as it relates to their sphere of work.

To fully protect yourself, you'll want to remember and follow four steps as it relates to each policy[6]:

- Implement
- Inform
- Train
- Enforce

I have had a handful of cases against professional drivers in my career where I represented an injured party who had been in a crash involving a semitruck, a news van, and in one case, a Grumman LLV (those odd-looking post-office delivery trucks).

In each of those cases where I sued the employer for direct negligence, that list above became my roadmap for success.

I would pull in the employer for a deposition and ask a series of questions aimed at discovering where the employer's failure occurred (and there always was one). For example, let's assume that I am asking questions in a case where a semitruck driver fell asleep at the wheel and ran my client off the road, and I believe he had been driving for far longer than is reasonable such that falling asleep would be foreseeable. I am going to ask questions designed to discover if the employer was taking appropriate steps to protect against this:

---

[6] *See, e.g., Fox v. Nu Line Transp. LLC,* No. 2:18-CV-00502, 2020 WL 4432869, at *1 (W.D. La. July 31, 2020), aff'd sub nom. *Fox v. Nu Line Transp., L.L.C.,* No. 20-30716, 2022 WL 3928525 (5th Cir. Aug. 31, 2022).

- What is your company policy related to the number of consecutive hours an employee can drive? What about total nonconsecutive hours in a day? How does that compare to the federal regulation?

- Was the truck driver in this case aware of that policy? How do you know? Did you give a written copy of the policy to the driver? If so, when did that happen? Have there been any updates to the policy since then? If so, did you provide a copy of the updated policy? Did you have the driver sign acknowledging it? Do you have a copy of that acknowledgment? Is the policy posted somewhere in the vehicle that the driver will regularly see it? Is it posted at your headquarters?

- When was the last time you trained on this policy? How often do you hold these trainings? And then for each of the training meetings:
    - What specific content related to this policy did you cover? Was the meeting mandatory? Was it in person? Do you have minutes from that meeting? Did you take attendance? Was this driver present?

- What steps did you take to enforce this policy? Do drivers keep a log of hours driven? Are there objective checks and balances you can use to verify the hours driven? Have you ever caught a driver violating the policy? What did you do? What about this driver? How many times? When is the last time you reviewed this driver's logs? Did it seem odd to you that the driver was able to get from Phoenix to Denver in less than ten hours? What is the range of a full tank of gas? Do drivers stop to use the restroom?

No employer wants to find themselves in a situation where their every action is being examined under a microscope. If that does ever happen, they're going to want to have good answers. Pull out your highlighter and start dog-earing these pages. Every doctor needs to evaluate their own business and observe the best practices laid out below.

Implement Appropriate Policies

When it comes to implementing policies at work, we're aiming for safety and protection. Protect our employees, our customers, and ourselves. Protect us from them, them from us, and them from each other. Virtually every law or contract relating to the workplace has some form of safety and protection in mind.[7]

Labor laws protect the employee from the employer. HIPAA laws protect the patient from us and our employees. The non-solicitation agreement protects us from our former employees. You get the idea.

Chances are you are not up to speed on the laws or even all the potential risks that are inherent to owning a practice and employing healthcare professionals. So how can you make sure your policies comply with all those legal requirements you don't know about?

The good news is, you don't have to know it all. Businesses that will do this work for you are plentiful.[8] As you do your due diligence to find these resources so you can implement proper policies in your workplace, you'll want to ensure you're not only covered on the broad policies that apply to every employer in your city and state,[9] but also those field-specific laws and regulations that apply to health care practices.

For example, whether you are a plumbing contractor or a medical professional, you must comply with minimum wage and overtime laws. But if you are a plumbing contractor,[10] you're also going to want to make sure your plumbers are familiar with local building code. If you are a medical professional,[11] you will be fully aware that your employees, from the receptionist answering the phones to the associate physician working Thursday nights and weekends, had better know HIPAA.

Although resources abound to help you adopt the right policies in your workplace, ultimately you're the one who is responsible for

---

[7] That's true of laws and contracts in general, not just in the workplace.

[8] I should know, I'm one of them. Incidentally, if you want to reach me, check me out at https://thefortunelawfirm.com.

[9] You have to comply with all the city, state, and federal labor laws applicable in your locale, regardless of whether you are aware of them. *Ignorantia juris non excusat*.

[10] If any plumbing contractors are reading this book, I would be amazed. And impressed. Also, I'll buy you lunch. Drop me a line.

[11] And based on the cover of the book alone, you're either a medical professional (it's in the title) or one of the author's close family members or friends showing support by reading something that doesn't apply to you and that you're not interested in at all. Either way, thank you. Your support means a lot.

making sure you're workplace policies are not only legally compliant, but also robust enough to protect you, your employees, and your patients.

Inform Your Employees of Those Policies

Once you've adopted the policies that will govern your practice, you need to make sure your employees are aware of them.

To inform your healthcare professionals of these policies, including them in the employee handbook is a no-brainer. When you hire a new RN or RDN, give them a copy of the handbook (or better yet, send them a digital copy or give them access to one online). Tell them reading it is mandatory and have them sign an acknowledgment that they received and read the handbook.

If you implement a new policy and update the handbook, make sure your existing healthcare professionals get a copy, read it, and acknowledge the receipt and review of the policy in writing.

You'll keep the signed acknowledgments in the employee's personnel file.

Some policies, like employee rights under the Fair Labor Standards Act, must be conspicuously posted in the workplace.[12] You may want to post others in simple terms where it will do the most good. For example, you might have a sign above your trash cans that says "Do Not Dispose of Needles and Other Sharps in the Garbage Can."

Be thoughtful about whether it makes sense to inform employees about a specific policy beyond their having access to the handbook. For most policies, the handbook is probably enough. Picture yourself in a deposition being challenged on whether your employees were properly informed on how to secure and maintain the confidentiality of patient medical records. Then take action to guarantee if that ever happens, you have a good answer.[13]

Train the Employees on Your Policies

Adopting a policy and informing your employees is not enough. You've got to keep it fresh in their minds through regular trainings. You may want to remind them of the content and processes for the

---

[12] U.S. Department of Labor, "Workplace Posters," available at https://www.dol.gov/general/topics/posters (last accessed January 25, 2023).
[13] For your convenience, some further ideas are provided below! Don't say I'm not making this legal stuff pretty easy.

informed consent protocols. Give examples of effective practice and poor practice. Let them ask questions. Create a culture where the policies are not to be endured, but embraced. Remember, they're there for safety and protection.

When you hold these training meetings, you'll want to take attendance. If it's an in-person meeting, have them sign an attendance sheet. If it's virtual, your web conference provider should have the capability of logging not just who attends, but what precise time they logged on and off. Consider recording the meeting.

Create an agenda for the meeting. Pull the policy out of the handbook and go over it directly. Or create a slideshow highlighting certain parts of it.

After the meeting, take the attendance roster, the meeting minutes, a link to the recording, a copy of the slide deck, and anything else you have created for the meeting and stick it wherever you keep your corporate records. This will help not only in terms of employee liability but also for corporate formalities.[14]

What constitutes "regular" is going to depend on your field, what kinds of employees you have (are they all administrative staff, or do you have licensed practitioners?), how many employees you have, how many offices, etc. I hold certain types of meetings annually, others quarterly, others monthly, and others weekly. You will be the best arbiter of what "regular" means in your workplace, and you can check in with other physicians to get a feel for what they do.

I once went to visit my chiropractor. While I was in the waiting room, I heard a female patient complaining to the receptionist about pain and discomfort, though she didn't get into specifics.

A few minutes later, as the receptionist was walking me back to the treatment room, she told me that the lady's pain was related to a breast-reduction surgery she'd recently had.

Alarm bells were going off in my head. This receptionist, who was not medically trained, did not have any licenses, and whose responsibilities were only marginally related to any sort of medical treatment (answering phones, checking people in, and walking the patients to the back), nonetheless had access to protected health information and was using it to fuel gossip about other patients.

She was violating HIPAA.

Who's to blame here? The culprit is most likely the chiropractor's insufficient (or perhaps non-existent) training.

---

[14] We'll discuss those in a later chapter.

Cover HIPAA frequently. That's something that an employee deals with every day. Make sure your employees know what the anti-harassment policy is, and how and to whom to report harassment. Do those trainings at least quarterly.

There is no limit to what policies to cover in these meetings. Cover all of them. Paid time off. Sick days. Overtime. Phone etiquette. How to check in a patient. Phone use while driving a company vehicle. If it's an expectation you have in the workplace, go over it now and again. Not only will clearer communications and well-delineated expectations make for a smoother work environment, it will also reduce the potential for both direct and vicarious liability.

Enforce the Policies

Policies do no good, no matter how well the employee understands them, if they are not enforced. An unenforced rule is no rule at all.

Unfortunately, enforcement is often the most difficult of these steps to implement. It's uncomfortable. Awkward.[15] Sometimes it's disruptive and expensive (like if you have to fire someone and find and train someone new). But enforcement is important because you want your patients to know, your employees to know, and that attorney deposing you to know, that the rules in your workplace, designed to protect people and keep them safe—they mean something.

Enforcement means consequences. If someone violates a policy, there must be a consequence. The scope of what that consequence can be may vary between jurisdictions, but keep in mind that consequence doesn't necessarily mean punishment. It could be a verbal admonition (which should be documented in their personnel file). Perhaps a written warning (have the employee sign acknowledging receipt). Or mandatory retraining.

The consequence should match the infraction. Repeated tardiness may result in reduction of hours, if that fits your needs, like pushing back their start time by an hour.

If your medical practice culture is such that your employees take turns participating in the regular trainings, you could ask if they'd be comfortable training on the subject at the next meeting (but don't do anything that would make them feel like you are trying to single them out or humiliate them).

---

[15] Doctors definitely have a head start in dealing with awkward conversations that might make others blush or pause.

It's not your job to train them to be a decent human being, and you're not their parent, but you have every right (and the responsibility) to make sure they are complying with the policies and rules in your practice. Particularly those that relate to safety or the law. If in doubt, consult your HR department or an employment attorney. And document everything![16]

Enforcement Sometimes Means Termination

One of the most difficult means of enforcement is terminating those employees who pose too big of a risk to your practice. This is difficult not only for the personal cost of letting someone go—telling them that they can no longer rely on you for a paycheck, and they'll have to find other means to support themselves, and where applicable, their families. But terminating an employee also has its own potential liabilities. If the justification for firing an employee is well reasoned and well documented, you should be safe, but if in doubt, consult an employment attorney.

I have employed several paralegals since opening my own practice. Many of them have been great. But I've had my share of duds, too.

Like a medical clinic, my law office also handles private information. HIPAA applies insofar as we are handling medical records of clients, and privilege always applies. And like doctors, we lawyers are ultimately responsible for our employees' breaches. So it is important that we hire the right people, make sure they know the rules, are trained on the rules, and that those rules are enforced.

There are only a few things that a lawyer is authorized that a paralegal cannot. Among those are (1) establishing the attorney-client relationship, (2) setting fees to be charged for legal services, and (3) signing pleadings.[17]

I had to fire the first paralegal I ever hired. The law firm was brand new, but these rules were well established. They were rules the paralegal knew and had been trained on.

We had very few clients when we first started, and to procure more clients, we started advertising that we would resolve traffic tickets for

---

[16] A.K.A channel your inner lawyer! If you need some tips, ask me.
[17] Model Rules of Professional Conduct 1.4 & 1.5; *see also* NALA Ethics Canon 3 and American Bar "ABA Model Guidelines for the Utilization of Paralegal Services," available at https://www.scbar.org/media/filer_public/2a/6a/2a6a8997-13fd-40c8-b208-e3210f4a99b4/ls_prlgs_modelguidelines.pdf at 9, last accessed November 9, 2023.

free. The idea was that we would establish relationships with people who would either recommend our firm or hire us in the future.[18]

Depending on the applicable court, that either meant sending fax negotiations to get them reduced to parking tickets[19] or, in some instances, appearing at court for a pro forma hearing where a handful of cases could be handled at once.

We held weekly meetings, part of which was dedicated to reviewing the calendar for the upcoming week. At one such meeting, the paralegal informed me that I had two different hearings on the same day in two different courthouses, one of which was about as far as you could drive from our office and still be in the same valley.

I looked at the names of the cases and didn't recognize them. The following conversation ensued:

"Who is this?"

"Oh, this is a traffic case."

"A traffic case? In North Las Vegas, I don't remember discussing that."

"Oh, he came in the other day. He has nine warrants out for his arrest."

"Arrest warrants? I don't know anything about resolving warrants. We don't do arrest warrants. We do traffic tickets, and we barely do those. I don't remember talking to him. I'm sure I would have turned him down."

"No, you didn't talk to him."

"If I didn't talk to him, then how is he a client?"

"Oh, I signed him up."

"You signed him up?"

"Yeah."

"And how much are we charging this client to resolve nine arrest warrants?"

"$400."

"$400?!"

"Yeah."

"How did you get hearings without filing a motion?"

"I filed a motion."

---

[18] If you were wondering, as a marketing idea, it didn't really work.

[19] If you're outside of Nevada, maybe you're thinking it's odd that moving violations can be reduced to expensive parking tickets as a matter of course. If you're from Nevada or another state where that's normal, perhaps you're just wondering how long ago this was if we were still using fax machines.

"I never signed a motion."
"No, I signed it for you."

As you can probably imagine, the conversation was not that straightforward. There was a lot more obfuscating, hemming, hawing, and stuttering. She knew what she had done was way over the line. For some reason, though, she thought it would be okay because she thought she was generating revenue for the firm.

I attended the hearings, and I honored the quoted price. And don't ask me how, but I got those arrest warrants removed. I don't know if the client realized it, but he got the best deal he could have possibly gotten.

And my paralegal lost her job. I needed to protect myself and my clients from that kind of reckless behavior.

You will need to make similar judgment calls. Your field and mine are high-stakes fields. Mistakes in my field can result in loss of property, livelihood, or freedom. Mistakes in yours can mean permanent injury or death.

Negligent retention is a tort that means you can directly be held legally liable for keeping employees on payroll that you should have fired.

The bottom line: fire bad employees. It's not just a good idea, it's the law.

PART II

Protecting Your Assets

CHAPTER 7

Introduction to Liability

For over a decade, I was a civil trial attorney. I held people liable for the damages they caused (and in some cases, I defended them). You could say I was a liability attorney.

Liability is one of those words that gets bandied about a lot, but I'm not sure most people really understand what it means. It seems to be a catch-all excuse for why someone is no fun or to explain a downer policy.

The McDonald's manager: "I'm sorry, we can't have older kids play in the ball pit for liability reasons."

The escape room owner: "You have to fill out waivers for your kids before anyone can play the room. It's for liability reasons."[1]

The person you've reached out to on an online dating platform: "I can't go out with you. For liability reasons."[2]

You've heard that phrase before—"for liability reasons." And you probably just nodded, accepting the explanation.[3]

---

[1] You can imagine the patience with which I respond to someone preaching liability to me. I understand liability. And I also understand that their rationale has more to do with their irrational fear than from any actual legal advice. I have learned to bite my tongue, even though in many states, including my own (Utah), waivers that parents sign on behalf of their minor children are legally ineffectual. They violate public policy of the state, and courts refuse to recognize them. *See, e.g., Taylor v. Taylor*, 2022 UT 35, 58, 517 P.3d 380, 393.

[2] Ouch. I made this up, by the way. I hope this has never happened to you.

[3] Next time you hear it, think about it in the context where you heard it. In at least 63% of cases where the phrase is used, it doesn't make sense. (That's not a real stat—I made that up, too. The real number is probably higher.)

Liability is the legal right to hold someone accountable for their actions by means of a court-ordered monetary award. It is a mechanism through which you can force someone to pay for the harm they've caused.[4]

When we talk about asset protection, we are typically talking about protection from liability in a civil court. Meaning, someone may get a judgment against you, but they don't get any of your possessions in satisfaction of that judgment. To understand asset protection, we need to understand what it would look like to be held liable in a civil court. Let me walk you through a very general timeline from the act that produces the wrong to the legal pronouncement of liability:

Step 1: *The harm-producing act.* This could be anything that causes (or that the plaintiff at least alleges causes) harm or loss to another, including physical harm (injury), emotional harm (emotional injury, including having to deal with an injury of a loved one), reputational harm (think libel or slander), financial harm (damage to property, lost wages), mental harm (pain and suffering), and even symbolic harm (where you may not have lost anything measurable, but your rights were nonetheless infringed, like in a simple trespass case). Examples of a harm-producing act in your practice could be a delayed diagnosis or a surgical error.

---

[4] That's not the legal definition. But it is one that makes sense. If I wanted to twist your mind in knots, I would have provided the one from *Black's Law Dictionary*:

1. The quality, state, or condition of being legally obligated or accountable; legal responsibility to another or to society, enforceable by civil remedy or criminal punishment <liability for injuries caused by negligence>. — Also termed *legal liability*; *subjection*; *responsibility.* Cf. fault. 2. (*often pl.*)A financial or pecuniary obligation in a specified amount; debt <tax liability> <assets and liabilities>.

"The term 'liability' is one of at least double signification. In one sense it is the synonym of *duty*, the correlative of *right*; in this sense it is the opposite of *privilege* or *liberty*. If a duty rests upon a party, society is now commanding performance by him and threatening penalties. In a second sense, the term 'liability' is the correlative of *power* and the opposite of *immunity.* In this case society is not yet commanding performance, but it will so command if the possessor of the power does some operative act. If one has a power, the other has a liability. It would be wise to adopt the second sense exclusively. Accurate legal thinking is difficult when the fundamental terms have shifting senses." William R. Anson, *Principles of the Law of Contract* 9 (Arthur L. Corbin ed., 3d Am. ed. 1919).

"Liability or responsibility is the bond of necessity that exists between the wrongdoer and the remedy of the wrong. This *vinculum juris* is not one of mere duty or obligation; it pertains not to the sphere of *ought* but to that of *must.*" John Salmond, *Jurisprudence* 364 (Glanville L. Williams ed., 10th ed. 1947).

LIABILITY, Black's Law Dictionary (11th ed. 2019)

Step 2: *Demand for recompense*. Often when some harm is done, or perceived to have been done, the putative victim will notify you. It may be they just want you to own up to your behavior with an apology. Perhaps they want you to pay for dental repairs, medical bills, or monetary damages. This step is not required to move forward but is usually part of the process because if the putative victim gets what they want here, they have expended very little money and effort, and if resolved in a matter satisfactory to you and the patient, both parties can move forward with your lives.

Step 3: *Litigation*. If step 2 fails, or if it is skipped, the putative victim can either drop the matter and move on or initiate litigation. To initiate litigation, they must serve you with summons and a complaint.[5] The putative victim has sued you, and now you've both got new titles. They are the plaintiff, and you are the defendant. In the complaint, they must notify you what legal claims they have for seeking recompense. These are identified in what are called claims or causes of action. They may be suing for negligence, defamation, breach of contract, or fraud. Different jurisdictions have different minimum standards that apply to the allegations, but at the very least, they must put you on notice of what claims are being brought against you.

Step 4: *Judgment*. Litigation is a long step and can take years. It involves a lot of fact gathering (subpoenas, depositions, written requests for information), motion work (asking the judge to require the other party to do something, including ending the case with a win for one party or another), and ultimately—if the case does not end prematurely through motion or settlement—a judgment, either by judicial decree (by motion or bench trial) or via verdict (jury trial).

Step 5: *Judgment Collection*. Once the plaintiff has a judgment in their favor, they are promoted from plaintiff to judgment creditor, and it's time to collect. If you have insurance that covers the amount of the judgment, then your insurance company pays and it's over.[6] If you don't, or if the amount of the judgment exceeds the policy limits, then the judgment creditor is coming after any possessions of yours that they can get their hands on. Your bank account, your investment accounts, investment properties, equity in your primary residence, your ATVs, skis, guns, stamps, jewelry, etc.

---

[5] Terminology may vary from jurisdiction to jurisdiction, but to my knowledge, if they don't all call them a summons and complaint, the vast majority do.
[6] That's called "indemnity."

So let's simplify this. If you are found liable, and a judgment is entered against you, the patient–plaintiff-judgment-creditor can now take all of your stuff that is not protected.

Those last four words, "that is not protected," is where we do our best work.

That's what asset protection is. It's organizing your life and businesses in such a way that your stuff (or at least as much of it as legally can be) is protected. Then, if the worst happens, even if someone wins a judgment against you, it won't be worth the paper it's written on. And if they can be convinced ahead of time that you're not worth coming after for that reason, then you may just head litigation off at the pass.[7]

So how do we do that? What does it look like to organize your life in such a way that your possessions are protected? It's the same way we protect your license. We look at the rules and then work within them. So let's look at three different categories of protection: (1) statutory protections that are built in, (2) protections created from the establishment of business entities, and (3) protections from trusts.

But first, a caveat.

Sidebar: Where Does Insurance Fit into This?

Let me put these asset protection strategies into context for you. Your first line of defense is going to be your liability insurance. There's a reason they call it *liability* insurance. It insures you against *liability*.

If you're a doctor,[8] you probably are the insured on at least four liability insurance policies: (1) your malpractice insurance, (2) premises liability insurance for the building you occupy for business, whether you own or rent it, (3) renters or homeowner's insurance for your primary residence, and, (4) car insurance.

Each of these policies is going to cover different potential harms. If someone slips on a wet floor in your office, it's the premises liability insurance. If you've been accused of medical negligence, it is your professional liability insurance (i.e., medical malpractice insurance). Hit someone with your car? Car insurance. You get how this works.

---

[7] Phew. No report to the NPDB—remember Part I? (Possibly, if you're not exhausted from work or just skipped over that bit! If the latter, go back. It's important.)
[8] If you are reading this and you're not a doctor, then you're probably my mom. Hi, Mom!

When you purchase liability insurance, the insurance company is very generally promising you at least two things: (1) to defend you if you ever get sued, and (2) to pay for any damages you've caused that are covered in the scope of your policy up to the limits of the policy. These are called, respectively, the duty to defend, and the duty to indemnify.[9]

So you might be wondering, if I have insurance, why would I need to engage in any other form of asset protection? If insurance is going to pay the damages, then I get to keep my assets, right?

In a perfect world, you would be right. That's all we'd need. Well, if the world were perfect, people would never suffer losses, and they wouldn't be accusing us of hurting them, so we wouldn't need insurance, either. We live in a very imperfect world. A world where liability insurance is not always enough.

There are several reasons liability insurance may fail as your first line of defense. Let me focus on three.

First, it may be that harm occurs outside the realm of anything you've purchased insurance for. If your dog attacks someone, for example.[10] If you're at a ball game and accidentally trip someone, and they get hurt, they could sue you for negligence, and any judgment resulting would not likely be covered by insurance. Damages for breach of contract, defamation, and intentional or criminal acts are typically not covered by liability insurance.

Second, it could be that an exclusion in your policy operates to excuse coverage. Insurance companies are happy to collect your money every month when the premium is due, but when it comes time to step up and pay, they're often reluctant to let go of their money. They'll point to this exclusion or that to justify why they won't pay.

Did you know that in your medical malpractice policy, there is likely a provision in there that requires you to report, not just claims, but any occurrence that may result in a claim? Meaning, any time there is an adverse outcome, or an upset patient whose outcome was not adverse but may have been somewhat less than optimal, the insurance contract[11] may require you to let them know.

If you don't notify your insurer, and the patient makes a claim several months or more later, and the insurance company finds out by reviewing the charts that you were aware of the potential for a claim,

---

[9] If you read footnote 6 in this chapter, then you already knew what indemnity was. Isn't learning fun?

[10] In some cases, that may be covered by your homeowner's or renter's insurance.

[11] The insurance contract, or policy, is that really long document you never read.

they could point to the notice paragraph and choose not to defend you. There are all sorts of little exclusionary paragraphs in your policy.

I had a case where I represented a woman who was seven months pregnant. She and her fiancé were parked in their car several blocks from her ex-husband's house. He was supposed to have dropped off their seven-year-old son earlier that day but had not. My client and her fiancé were waiting for the police to arrive to monitor the custody exchange because ex-husband was apparently scary.

The police were in no hurry, and after more than an hour of waiting, ex-husband drove by the couple on his way home and saw them there, parked in their car. He drove home, switched vehicles to one that was unregistered and uninsured, then came back.

He sped towards their parked car as if he was going to ram the driver's side of the vehicle, then screeched to a halt. Without word or preamble, he jumped out of the car brandishing a billy club, forced the driver's side door open, pulled the fiancé out, and started beating him.

My client, who had dialed 9-1-1, was not sure how to give the police directions to where they were parked as she didn't know the street name. The dispatcher asked her to get out of the car and see if she could see street signs that would provide a clue they could use to send the police to the right location. She was just a few steps out of the car when ex-husband, who had gotten back in his vehicle, put it in reverse and drove into her, knocking her down. Then he drove over her with the rear tire, shifted into drive, and drove over her again.

Luckily, despite his best efforts, both my client and her unborn baby survived. Baby girl was none the worse for the wear, born healthy and beautiful two months later. Mom suffered some broken bones, burns, and scrapes, but recovered physically, although she has scarring and undoubtedly still suffers from the trauma. Fiancé eventually regained his physical health, too, despite the beating.

The vehicle was uninsured, so there was going to be no insurance from ex-husband. He didn't have any assets to speak of and wasn't making enough at his new job hammering out license plates in prison to make a dent in their damages, so although we sued him and got a judgment against him, our main case was against my client's insurance company.

My client's fiancé was the owner of the vehicle they were in, and he had the foresight to purchase uninsured motorist coverage, which covers vehicle-related injuries caused by uninsured motorists.

Notwithstanding the policy, and its willingness to collect premiums for years without complaint, the insurance company denied coverage for two reasons: (1) she and fiancé were not married, so she wasn't covered by his insurance, and (2) she had stepped out of the vehicle when she was hit.

The justifications for denial were ridiculous. They knew it, their attorney knew it, and I knew it. My clients didn't understand it. They were traumatized by the event and thought they would be covered. And because they had been paying for that coverage for so long and assumed they were purchasing something with all those premiums, they were justified in believing it.

At one point, the insurance company's attorney took my client's deposition, trying to get her to admit absurdities that they felt would justify their unfounded position. He had to end the deposition early because my client was so emotional and couldn't answer through the sobbing.

The insurance company dragged the case out for years. There were times I would meet with the client, and she would bring her daughter, who had grown into a toddler. At a certain point, the insurance company's attorneys started apologizing to me for the case. They didn't understand the insurance company's position any more than I did. This was obviously not a case with good optics for the insurance company, and it wouldn't make any sense to take it to trial, but they doggedly persisted anyway. It wasn't until just before trial that the insurance company finally settled.

This was just one personal experience I had. But it happens all the time. Look up "liability insurance bad faith" for examples that abound of insurance companies denying coverage to their insureds based on some language in the policy, which is often twisted or distorted to their benefit.

That's the second reason liability insurance may be an inefficient first line of defense: your insurance company may, for reasons that may or may not be justified, refuse the coverage you've purchased.

The third way liability insurance could fail is if the coverage you purchased is insufficient to pay the judgment.

I just spoke to a doctor yesterday who is two years into a medical malpractice lawsuit. The plaintiff is alleging seven figures of damages, most of which derive from her lost wages claim.

The doctor has only $200,000 in liability limits because at some point, some knuckle-dragger posing as an insurance expert told him that having high liability limits puts a target on your back, and that having low liability limits deters litigation.[12] In the meantime, the doctor has millions of dollars of unprotected assets. Those assets are now at risk because the doctor moved the target from his insurance company to himself.[13]

Telling someone with high net worth to keep their liability limits low is like telling a frontline soldier to carry a small shield because it makes a smaller target for the enemy.

You don't have to have low liability coverage for this to apply. Go peruse the outcomes listed on page 47 to see some recent verdicts of two colleagues of mine, and then call your insurance company to see what the premiums would be to get that much coverage.

So why do we employ asset-protection strategies beyond just purchasing insurance? Because in a world where insurance companies look for any excuse not to provide coverage, and plaintiffs look for every way to increase their potential damages,[14] we don't want to leave our futures in the hands of the insurance companies and the plaintiffs—two parties whose interests do not align with yours. We've got to have a backup plan.

So, before we got sidetracked by this where-does-insurance-fit-in sidebar, I was going to show you three different categories of protection: (1) statutory protections that are built in (chapter 8), (2) protections created from the establishment of business entities (chapters 9–12[15]), and (3) protections from trusts (chapter 13). We'll get to that now.

---

[12] Although rules vary from jurisdiction to jurisdiction, in many cases, the plaintiff doesn't know what your liability limits are until after they file a lawsuit. In those jurisdictions, the amount of liability protection you have is going to have zero effect on the plaintiff's behavior. Also, $200,000 is still a lot of reasons to file a lawsuit, even if the plaintiff thinks that's all they will ever get.
[13] It makes me shudder to think of all the different ways bad advice can harm people.
[14] It's odd, but when I represented the defendants, the plaintiffs were always faking or exaggerating. When I represented the plaintiffs, the defense always stubbornly refused to pay even though the claims were valid and free of hyperbole. I guess I just got lucky to always be representing the right side.
[15] Four chapters! That's a hint this is an important approach.

CHAPTER 8

Built-in Statutory Protections

Some of your assets may already be protected without you knowing it. Every state has protections designed to ensure creditors cannot take so much that you end up homeless or unable to support yourself or your family either during your working years or during retirement.

These exemption laws vary greatly, depending on what state you live in, but as a general rule, every state is going to have exemptions for the following:[1]

- Equity in your home
- Equity in a vehicle
- Tools of your trade
- Part of your unpaid wages
- Clothing
- Household goods
- A portion of your bank account
- Government benefits like welfare and unemployment

---

[1] CFPB, "Can a Debt Collector Take or Garnish My Wages or Benefits?" Consumer Financial Protection Bureau, August 2, 2024, available at https://www.consumerfinance.gov/ask-cfpb/can-a-debt-collector-take-or-garnish-my-wages-or-benefits-en-1439/, last accessed November 9, 2023.

Some states will also protect much more than that, including firearms, jewelry, private libraries, works of art, among other things.[2]

In some cases, those protections will be built in and require no action on your part. In others, you may be required to file a document or get a court order to enable it.

Homestead Protection

The protection you have in your home is called the homestead exemption. Except for New Jersey and Pennsylvania, every state has made at least some portion of the equity in your home off-limits to creditors. If you live in Florida,[3] Iowa,[4] Kansas,[5] Oklahoma,[6] South Dakota,[7] or Texas,[8] all the equity in your home is protected.

To know the homestead limits in your state, just google "[your state] homestead limits." Sometimes it is a single number, sometimes it varies based on certain factors, like whether you are married or the median home price in your county.[9] In New York, the limits depend on what county you live in and whether you are married.[10]

The homestead typically only applies to a single personal residence, so if you have multiple homes, usually only one will have homestead protection.[11] It often requires the filing of a declaration of homestead with the county recorder to be effective, though that's not always something you have to do until your home is under threat of foreclosure.[12]

---

[2] *See, e.g.,* NRS 21.090. Louisiana will protect "one utility trailer," "the family portraits," and "all dogs, cats, and other household pets." But only one cow. La. Rev. Stat. § 13:3881.
[3] Fla. Stat. § 222.01–02, Fla. Const. Art. X § 4.
[4] Iowa Code § 561.16.
[5] Kan. Stat. § 60-2301.
[6] 31 Okl. St. § 2.
[7] S.D. Cod. Laws § 43-45-3.
[8] Tex. Const. Art. XVI §§ 50–51; Tex. Prop. Code § 41.001–002.
[9] *E.g.,* Ca. Civ. Proc. Code § 704.730.
[10] N.Y. Civ. Prac. L. and R. § 5206(a).
[11] Utah, though, allows $5,000 in homestead protection for investment properties that are not your personal residence (double that if you're married). Utah Code § 78B-5-503(2).
[12] *See, e.g.,* Utah Code § 78B-5-504(1).

Social Security Payments and Other Government Benefits

Government benefits like social security, disability, and unemployment also enjoy privileged status when it comes to creditor protection.[13] Those are typically[14] completely off-limits.

Private Retirement Accounts

Private retirement accounts, too, like 401(k)s, IRAs, and other retirement plans made possible by the tax code are also asset protected, though some states place limits on that protection.[15]

Most states provide unlimited protection to retirement funds in normal circumstances. Exceptions are routinely made, though, allowing the otherwise protected funds to be garnished to pay alimony,[16] child support,[17] amounts contributed within the last 90 days,[18] 120 days,[19] or one year,[20] or three years,[21] judgments for contract claims,[22] judgments for felonious killings,[23] among other variations.

Some states place caps on what is protected. Minnesota only protects $69,000 plus what might reasonably be necessary to provide support for the debtor and their family.[24] Maine is $15,000 plus that

---

[13] 42 U.S.C. § 407(a).

[14] Typically, as in, I have never heard of an exception but don't want to speak in absolutes.

[15] Read the first third of my book, *Unshackled: How to Escape the Chains of Conventional Wisdom that Keep You Poor*, if you want my unfettered analysis of why it is always a bad idea to put money into a non-Roth retirement account like a 401(k) or IRA.

[16] La. Rev. Stat. §§ 20:3(1) and 13:3881(D)(1).

[17] *E.g.*, Ky. Rev. Stat. § 427.150(2)(f).

[18] N.Y.C.P.L.R. 5205(c).

[19] Alaska Stat. § 09.38.017.

[20] La. Rev. Stat. §§ 20:33(1) and 13:3881(D)(1).

[21] Haw. Rev. Stat. § 651-124.

[22] Ark. Code §16-66-220.

[23] Colo. Rev. Stat. § 13-54-102. This exception might well have been a response to the OJ Simpson civil trial. The family of Ron Goldman sued OJ Simpson for wrongful death, and won, but were largely unable to collect on their judgment because his assets were all wrapped up in his NFL pension. "Goldman Won't Go After Simpson's Pension," CNN.com, August 28, 1997, available at http://www.cnn.com/US/9708/28/simpson.pension/, last accessed November 9, 2023.

[24] Minn. Stat. § 550.37(24).

necessary to provide support.[25] Nebraska's and California's exemption rules are completely situation specific, and the amount protected is that which is necessary to provide support now and through retirement, taking into account all other sources of income.[26] North Dakota protects up to $100,000 per account, or $200,000 total for all accounts.[27] Nevada only protects up to $500,000.[28] South Dakota puts their limit at $1 million.[29]

Most states do not protect inherited IRAs, though Florida,[30] North Carolina,[31] Ohio,[32] South Carolina,[33] and Texas[34] do.

Every state has their own rules about what is exempt, and the rules are easy to find online.[35]

Permanent Life Insurance

The cash value and death benefit associated with a permanent life insurance contract are also afforded protection, though like everything else, it is to varying degrees, depending on your state.

Most states (32 of them) will protect both the cash value and death benefit without any upper limits, though often it will only apply to seasoned contributions (e.g., those made at least a year ago), or in cases where the beneficiary is not the policy owner (which is almost always going to be true).[36]

On the low end of those protections are Connecticut and Maine, which only protect $4,000 of the cash value;[37] North Dakota and West

---

[25] Me. Rev. Stat. tit. 14 § 4422(13)(F).
[26] Cal. Code Civ. Proc. § 704.115; Neb. Rev. Stat. § 25-1663.01.
[27] N.D. Cent. Code § 28-22-03.1(7).
[28] NRS 21.090(1)(r).
[29] S.D. Cod. L. 43-45-16; 43-45-17.
[30] Fla. Stat. § 222.21.
[31] N.C. Gen. Stat. § 1C-1601(a)(9).
[32] Ohio Rev. Code § 2329.66(A)(10).
[33] S.C. Code § 15-43-30.
[34] Tex. Prop. Code § 42.0021.
[35] This is a nifty page I used for a lot of the information in this chapter: Asset Protection Planners "IRA Creditor Protection by State," available at https://www.assetprotectionplanners.com/planning/ira-by-state, last accessed March 1, 2023.
[36] *E.g.*, Va. Code § 38.2-3122(1) and (3).
[37] Ct. Gen. Stat. § 52-352b(s); 14 M.R.S. § 1422.

Virginia, which protect $8,000;[38] and Minnesota, which protects $9,600.[39]

These protections don't apply universally and often depend on your family situation.[40]

Any robust asset-protection plan should start with an analysis of what is already protected and where there might be room to move assets from unprotected to protected status.

For example, having worked hard to establish and run your dental or medical practice, you might have $300,000 of liquid cash that you want to protect. You live in a state with an unlimited homestead protection and have at least $300,000 left on your mortgage.

In these circumstances, you could put the money into equity in your home, and it would be protected (assuming the move is not made in response to a creditor, in which case that would be a fraudulent conveyance and ineffective; we'll talk more about that later).

Asset protection does not happen in a vacuum, though. Putting money somewhere where it's protected may come at the cost of higher taxes or lost investment opportunities. Your $300,000 can certainly work harder for you than paying off some mortgage interest. But if asset protection were your primary concern, that might make sense.

As I tell the doctors I work with, different asset-protection strategies come with different advantages and disadvantages that will need to be explored before you decide which, if any, might work best for you. So let's delve into some of the strategies that aren't built into your state's laws.

---

[38] N.D. Code § 261-33-36; W.Va. Code § 38-10-4(h).
[39] Minn. Stat. § 550.37(23).
[40] For a full list of states, along with references to the applicable statutes, see Gibbs, S. January 7, 2023, "Life Insurance Creditor Protection by State [Is your Cash Value and Death Benefit Covered?]" available at https://www.insuranceandestates.com/life-insurance-creditor-protection-by-state, last accessed March 1, 2023.

CHAPTER 9

Protecting Yourself with a Business Entity

If you own your own practice, chances are you are operating out of some form of business entity, even if you don't completely understand why. And if you are like roughly 60% of the doctors I ask, you aren't even entirely sure what kind of entity you have.

If you think your entity is an S-corp, then you are one of many that doesn't fully understand. But that's okay. You're reading this book. So you'll understand soon enough.

A Brief History of the Corporation and Limited Liability Company

Let's start with a basic review of the history of business entities. As a doctor, you might not feel that's history you need to consider. However, it provides a critical (and interesting) backdrop to our discussion of which sort of company to establish for your healthcare business. Like everything else, different states have different options, so we'll stick with the ones you can get pretty much everywhere: the corporation and the limited liability company, or LLC.[1]

---

[1] There are variations of these entities. A corporation, for example, can be a closely-held corporation, a personal holding company, or a personal service corporation. IRS.gov, September 2, 2022, "Frequently Asked Questions," available at https://www.irs.gov/faqs/small-business-self-employed-other-business/entities/entities-5, last accessed March 2, 2023. They can also be publicly or privately held. You may also see variations of the LLC, like the Series LLC or PLLC. We'll get into those a little bit later.

Limited liability arrangements have been around in some form for over a thousand years.[2] These arrangements, which resembled today's partnerships, evolved into joint-stock companies in the 1600s, then government-chartered corporations in the British colonies that would become the United States in the 1700s, to private corporations in the 1800s.[3] For hundreds of years, the only option for limited liability was the corporation, though most didn't have the resources to start or maintain one. And since corporations, by default, are double taxed (or at least have been since federal income taxes were implemented in 1913),[4] the limited liability it offered often wasn't worth the cost. Every small business owner who was not part of a corporation was personally liable for the debts and obligations of their business, but at least they were only paying taxes once.

Limited liability companies, although far more common now than corporations,[5] have only been around in their current form since 1997, though the story starts two decades before then.

The Hamilton Brothers Oil Company, a U.S. company based in Colorado, had been doing business overseas in the 1970s and had become familiar with a Panamanian entity (the limitada) that had both limited liability and pass-through (i.e., single-pay) taxation.[6] However, because they were concerned that the U.S. might not recognize those protections if they came from a foreign entity, they devised a scheme to bring such an entity to the U.S.[7]

The attorneys and accountants working for the oil company[8] drafted proposed legislation and took it to Alaska, where they felt the

---

[2] Hillman, RW. "Limited Liability in Historical Perspective," 54 *Wash. & Lee L. Rev.* 615, 621 (1997).

[3] Halloran, T. "A Brief History of the Corporate Form and Why It Matters," *Fordham J. Corp. Fin. Law*, (2018), available at https://news.law.fordham.edu/jcfl/2018/11/18/a-brief-history-of-the-corporate-form-and-why-it-matters, last accessed April 20, 2023.

[4] Hamill, SP. "The Origins Behind the Limited Liability Company," 59(5) *Ohio State Law Journal*, 1461 (1998).

[5] FLB Law. March 22, 2021, "Is It Time to Think About an LLC for Your Business?", available at https://www.flblaw.com/is-it-time-to-think-about-an-llc-for-your-business, last accessed April 20, 2023 (estimating 21.6 million LLCs and 1.7 million C-corporations).

[6] Hamill "The Origins Behind the Limited Liability Company," at 1463; WyomingLLCs.com, "The Complete History of the LLC," available at https://www.wyomingllcs.com/history-of-the-llc, last accessed April 20, 2023.

[7] WyomingLLCs.com "The Complete History of the LLC."

[8] Let's be honest, it was undoubtedly the attorneys who did all the work. The

oil-rich state would adopt it to protect the many oil companies working within its borders.[9] The legislation didn't take, losing a vote in 1975 and 1976.[10] Instead of trying a third time, Hamilton Brothers went to Wyoming, where the Cowboy State passed the law without vacillating.[11] Thus, in 1977, the LLC was born.[12]

There now existed an entity with complete limited liability that did not require incorporation and, on its surface, would allow for taxation as a partnership.[13] However, because uncertainty remained about whether the IRS would allow the partnership taxation, there was still work to be done.[14]

In the next ten years, due to the uncertainty regarding LLC taxation (the IRS promised it was looking into the issue and would get back to us shortly[15]) very few businesses[16] registered as an LLC (Hamilton Brothers wasn't even one of them), and only Florida followed in Wyoming's footsteps by establishing the LLC as a form of business organization.[17]

In 1988, though, the IRS issued a ruling definitively answering the question of how LLCs would be taxed.[18] The ruling allowed LLCs to be taxed as a partnership, rather than double taxed like a corporation.[19] This was a huge win for small business owners.

With the LLC, we now had a business entity that provided limited liability without double taxation. However, there was a flaw in the Wyoming law that the Hamilton Brothers had not foreseen when they proposed it: the LLC was very inflexible, making it difficult for the LLC

---

accountants were probably in the boardroom naysaying every idea with a monotone statement about numbers and balance sheets that didn't accomplish anything but making the meetings feel longer.

[9] WyomingLLCs.com "The Complete History of the LLC."
[10] *Id.*
[11] Wyo. Stat. §§ 17-15-100–17-15-144. *See also* Hamill at 1465.
[12] WyomingLLCs.com "The Complete History of the LLC."
[13] There were limited partnerships at the time, but in a limited partnership, there still has to be at least one designated partner, the general partner, who will assume the debts of the company. To get true limited liability, the general partner had to be a corporation, which to some extent defeated the purpose of a limited partnership, since the owners had to choose between assuming liability or creating a corporation, and if they were going to have a corporation anyway, why create the partnership?
[14] WyomingLLCs.com "The Complete History of the LLC."
[15] Hamill, "The Origins Behind the Limited Liability Company," at 1469.
[16] Less than 100. *Id.*
[17] WyomingLLCs.com "The Complete History of the LLC."
[18] Revenue Ruling 88-76, 1988-2 C.B. 360.
[19] WyomingLLCs.com "The Complete History of the LLC."

to transfer assets or to exist in perpetuity, so the Wyoming LLC was only a viable option for a few small business owners.[20]

These drawbacks served to prevent small businesses from registering as an LLC, but to modify the law to remove them would risk IRS-backtracking and the potential loss of the favored tax status.[21]

Over the next ten years, a concerted effort was made to draft legislation that every state could adopt that would allow greater flexibility.[22] At the same time, pressure was being put on the IRS to continue to allow favored tax treatment.[23] It wasn't until 1996, after every state had passed legislation allowing the formation of LLCs that the IRS finally passed its final ruling regarding taxation.[24] That rule became effective January 1, 1997, and that's the rule still in effect today.[25]

Corporation v. Limited Liability Company – Which One Is Better?

If you own a healthcare or other business, at some point you have been or will be faced with a choice of which type of entity to use for your business. And although one entity is not inherently or universally better than another, different entities fit different needs. So let's explore the attributes of both (spoiler: one of them is almost certainly better for you).

There are two major considerations you need to make before deciding which entity to use for your business, and not surprisingly, both have to do with money: first, what will it take to get complete limited liability? And second, which will give you the most advantageous tax treatment?

These are the same considerations the Hamilton Brothers had when trying to form their perfect entity. They didn't want to have to

---

[20] Hamill "The Origins Behind the Limited Liability Company," at 1470 (The Wyoming LLC rendered "interests in an LLC very difficult to transfer and the LLC itself highly dissolvable, limited the practical use of LLCs to small, closely held businesses and joint ventures.")

[21] *Id.*

[22] *Id.*

[23] *Id.*

[24] *Id.* The ruling, dubbed the "Check-the-Box" regulation because it allowed LLC owners to choose their taxation by checking a box on a form, was enacted on December 17, 1996. Treas. Reg. §§ 301.7701-1-4 (1996).

[25] *Id.* § (f).

choose between limited liability and favorable tax treatment. They wanted both.

If you establish your medical business as an LLC, then the owners are called members, and their ownership comes in the form of membership shares.[26] Certain formalities must be observed to maintain the LLC and preserve the separation between business and personal assets that forms the basis of an LLC's asset protection.[27] However, the rules and management of an LLC are very flexible.

Owners of a corporation are called shareholders and own the business through shares of issued stock.[28] A corporation must have a board of directors[29] and has more rigorous maintenance requirements than an LLC.[30]

Both the LLC and corporation will protect an owner's assets from the company liabilities,[31] and vice versa (assuming the entity is property set up and maintained—more on that in the next chapter).

The Tax Election

Business entities can be confusing because we often conflate the entity itself with the tax status or tax election of that entity, so let me try to make this simple.

When establishing your healthcare business, you can choose to form and do business out of a corporation or an LLC.[32]

---

[26] IRS.gov. "Limited Liability Company," January 25, 2023, available at https://www.irs.gov/businesses/small-businesses-self-employed/limited-liability-company-llc, last accessed March 2, 2023.
[27] We will cover that in great detail in the next chapter.
[28] IRS.gov. "Forming a Corporation," February 3, 2023, available at https://www.irs.gov/businesses/small-businesses-self-employed/forming-a-corporation, last accessed March 2, 2023.
[29] *E.g.*, Utah Code § 16-10a-801; Hawaii Rev. Stat. § 414-191(a).
[30] Watts, R. & Haskins, J. "LLC v. Corporation," Forbes.com, August 1, 2022, available at https://www.forbes.com/advisor/business/llc-versus-corporation/, last accessed March 2, 2023.
[31] *E.g.*, NRS 78.747(1), "No stockholder, director or officer of a corporation is individually liable for a debt or liability of the corporation, unless the stockholder, director or officer acts as the alter ego of the corporation"; "Pursuant to NRS 86.371 and NRS 86.381, a member cannot be personally responsible for the LLC's liabilities solely by virtue of being a member." *Gardner v. Henderson Water Park, LLC*, 133 Nev. 391, 392, 399 P.3d 350 (2017).
[32] Partnerships and sole proprietorships are an option, too, though those are beyond the scope of our discussion here. All four will generally be available anywhere you do

Your choice in business entity does not determine how that business will be taxed. An LLC, for example, can choose to be taxed as a corporation, a partnership, or as a disregarded entity.[33] A corporation is taxed as a C-corp by default or can make the S-election for tax purposes and become an S-corp.[34]

An LLC can also make the S-election.[35] Or it can choose to be taxed as a partnership or a disregarded entity.[36]

If you have an S-corp, what that really means is you have a corporation or an LLC that has made the S-election for tax purposes.

A C-corp pays taxes itself. Then you pay taxes separately on any income you make from the C-corp.[37] This is what we mean when we say you are double taxed if you own a C-corp. An S-corp, on the other hand, does not pay taxes. It files and reports to the IRS, but any profits from the business get included in your personal tax returns, and you only pay taxes once.[38]

Well, I tried to keep it simple! Although how you're taxed is important—we're going to come onto that in Part III—all you need to remember for now is that tax status isn't the key element in asset protection.

How Business Entities Protect Your Assets

The number one rule of asset protection is to keep your assets separate from your liabilities. That's almost the only rule that matters, actually. And although the legal means to accomplish this can be daunting to the uninitiated, in principle, it really is that simple.

---

business, though state by state you will see variations. For example, several states have a special type of LLC called a Series LLC. Others have a professional designation in PLLC.

[33] IRS.gov, "Limited Liability Company (LLC)," available at https://www.irs.gov/businesses/small-businesses-self-employed/limited-liability-company-llc, last accessed April 12, 2023.

[34] *See, e.g.,* IRS.gov, "S Corporations," available at https://www.irs.gov/businesses/small-businesses-self-employed/s-corporations, last accessed April 12, 2023.

[35] *See* IRS Form 8832, Entity Classification Election, available at https://www.irs.gov/pub/irs-pdf/f8832.pdf, last accessed April 12, 2023.

[36] *Id.*

[37] IRS.gov, "Forming a Corporation," available at https://www.irs.gov/businesses/small-businesses-self-employed/forming-a-corporation, last accessed April 12, 2023.

[38] IRS.gov, "S Corporations," last accessed April 12, 2023.

When you set up an LLC or other business entity to protect your assets, all it is doing is creating *separateness* between personal assets and business liabilities and between business assets and personal liabilities (or by separating one business's assets and liabilities from the assets and liabilities of another).

Consider this scenario: several years ago, you walked into Circuit City during their closeout sale to buy the latest Nickelback album. The sliding door at the entrance is malfunctioning, though, and it closes on you, injuring you.

You realize that Circuit City is going bankrupt, so you sue Best Buy instead. Best Buy is a healthy business that also sells electronics, so you'd rather get money from their bank account than from Circuit City's.

That's absurd, right? You can't collect from Best Buy on liabilities imposed by Circuit City. That much should be obvious. It's because they are separate entities. There is no confusion or question that Best Buy is responsible for its own actions and not Circuit City's. Likewise, Best Buy's assets are not available to satisfy Circuit City's debts.

But what if you wanted to collect from the Wurtzel family, the owners of Circuit City? Even though their company was going under, you found out that, as individuals, they still had millions.

You can't do that, either, unless you can prove that they hadn't been following the rules or properly maintaining their entity (the subject of the next chapter). That's precisely why they set up the corporation Circuit City Stores, Inc.: to keep liability separate. It was so separate that you probably had never heard of Sam or Alan Wurtzel.

But that's exactly what we're doing when we set up our own business entity, even if it is on a much smaller scale.

When you create a business entity, you are creating a new "person" in the law. This has been true for 200 years: "That corporations are, in law, for civil purposes, deemed persons, is unquestionable."[39] This law

---

[39] *United States v. Amedy*, 24 U.S. 392, 412, 6 L. Ed. 502 (1826).

has since been expanded to include limited liability companies.[40] They, too, are people under the law.[41]

And since one person generally cannot be held liable for the acts of another,[42] your LLC and you personally have separate liabilities. The protection is often written right into state statute:

> Nevada: "Except as otherwise specifically provided by statute or agreement, no person other than the limited-liability company is individually liable for a debt or liability of the limited-liability company unless the person acts as the alter ego of the limited-liability company."[43]

> Ohio: "A person who is a member of a limited liability company is not liable, solely by reason of being a member, for a debt, obligation, or liability of the limited liability company or a series thereof, whether arising in contract, tort, or otherwise."[44]

There are limitations to these protections, of course. First, your personal assets are protected only insofar as (1) it is your business that incurs the liability, and (2) your business is set up and maintained correctly.

The Krocs and the Waltons aren't worried about losing their riches if someone gets hurt at McDonald's or Walmart because when liability at one of their locations arises, it is always going to be related to something the business did or did not do. That's true for them because

---

[40] *See, e.g., Montgomery v. eTreppid Techs., LLC*, 548 F.Supp.2d 1175, 1181 (D. Nev. 2008); Cal. Corp. Code § 17703.04(b) (West 2014); Colo. Rev. Stat. § 7-80-107(1) (2017) (applying caselaw that interprets the conditions and circumstances under which the corporate veil of a corporation may be pierced under Colorado law to LLCs); *LD Prods., Ltd. v. Tech. Plastics of Or., LLC*, No. 05-556-KI, 2006 WL 3628062, at *3 (D. Or. Dec. 11, 2006); *Westmyer v. Flynn*, 382 Ill.App.3d 952, 321 Ill.Dec. 406, 889 N.E.2d 671, 678 (2008); *Howell Contractors, Inc. v. Berling*, 383 S.W.3d 465, 467-69 (Ky. Ct. App. 2012) (recognizing piercing of veil for an LLC in cases of fraud, illegality, or other unlawfulness); *Bottom Line Equip., LLC v. BZ Equip.*, LLC, 60 So.3d 632, 636 (La. Ct. App. 2011).

[41] *See, e.g., Dexxon Digital Storage, Inc. v. Haenszel*, 2005-Ohio-3187, 67, 161 Ohio App. 3d 747, 757, 832 N.E.2d 62, 70.

[42] There are exceptions, as you saw earlier in the book. Employers can be liable for the actions of their employees, for example. Parents can also be held liable for the actions of their minor children.

[43] NRS 86.376.

[44] ORC 1706.26.

you aren't going to see a member of the Walton family mopping the floor in the produce aisle and leaving behind a trail of slippery suds.

That's not necessarily true in your case, though.

If you are like most medical-professional business owners, you not only own your business, but you are also working at the business. Which means if you are excising a molar, prescribing medication, or performing surgery, and something goes wrong (or there is a perception that it did), the patient is not going to look to your corporation or LLC for recompense. They are going to look to you.

That's why the license protection measures we discussed in Part I are so important in your field. Because although the business entity you set up for your medical practice may well insulate you from its own liabilities, it does very little to protect you from the patients that you have personally treated.[45] And in your case, your potential business liabilities are probably slim.

That's also why you need more asset protection than business owners in almost any other industry: when your customer base perceives that they are harmed, they blame you because you're the one who actually touched them. They don't blame your business. They may not even know the name of their business.

That's not to say that having an LLC doesn't provide protection. If a patient comes after you personally and not the business, and they get a judgment against you, they may be able to take unprotected personal assets, but they cannot take your business's assets. The protection that *separateness* provides goes both ways.

If you have more than one medical practice—perhaps you run a family practice and a med spa—or if you invest in real estate or have other non-medical businesses on the side, having a separate entity for each is going to be critical not only to protect each business from each other and you from the businesses, but to protect the businesses from your personal liabilities.

So although an LLC may not provide the same insulation for you as it does for other businesses whose owners do not personally interact with their clients, it still keeps the LLC assets separate from each other and from your personal liabilities.

---

[45] Although a plaintiff in a case against Walmart could very well go after the employee who mopped the floor improperly, they probably aren't going to because Walmart is vicariously liable for the actions of its employees and has much deeper pockets. In your case, the perception is that you are the one with the deep pockets, so if they sue your entity at all, it will be secondary. You're going to be the first defendant.

Remember, where there is legal *separateness*, there is liability protection.

It makes sense that they can't take the LLC assets if they have a judgment against you, but what about taking the LLC itself? If they can take your stuff, and you own the LLC, why can't they take your ownership interest in the LLC?

Most states have some version of a law that prevents just that.[46] It's called charging order protection. These laws say something like this: "A judgment creditor's exclusive remedy against an LLC owned by the judgment debtor is a charging order allowing the judgment creditor to intercept dividends the LLC would otherwise distribute to the judgment creditor."[47]

The purpose behind this rule is to protect the business. If you incur personal liability, your judgment creditor will not be able to take action that will shut down the business. It also protects your partners, who have done nothing to incur any liability against this creditor. If your judgment creditor could seize ownership of your share of the business, then your partners would find themselves in business with someone they never wanted to be in business with, who may not know anything about the business, and whom your partners don't know and probably (after your experience with them) don't particularly like.

And while most states will extend charging order protection to LLCs with more than one owner, most do not. A Colorado bankruptcy court considered the issue and was unequivocal regarding the purpose of the protection:

> [T]he charging order ... exists to protect other members of an LLC from having involuntarily to share governance responsibilities with someone they did not choose, or from having to accept a creditor of another member as a co-manager. A charging order protects the autonomy of the original members and their ability to manage their own enterprise. In a single-member entity, there are no non-debtor members to protect. The charging order limitation serves no

---

[46] Bishop, CG. "Fifty State Series: LLC Charging Order Statute Table," 10-03 *Suffolk University Law School Research Paper* (2021). Available at SSRN: https://ssrn.com/abstract=1542244, last accessed April 20, 2023.

[47] Kagan, J. "Charging Order," *Investopedia*, January 26, 2023, available at https://www.investopedia.com/terms/c/charging-order.asp, last accessed April 20, 2023. *See, e.g.,* NRS 86.401 (Nevada's charging order statute).

purpose in a single member limited liability company, because there are no other parties' interests affected.[48]

In fact, only five states provide charging order protection for single-member LLCs (i.e., in situations where there is no innocent partner to protect): Alaska, Delaware, Nevada, South Dakota, and Wyoming.[49]

This protection typically applies to LLCs and partnerships. Nevada is the only state that grants charging order protection to corporations, too (elsewhere, your shares of a corporation can be seized by your creditor).[50]

The importance of this protection cannot be overstated: for LLCs formed in all but five states, to prevent your personal creditors from taking your business from you, you have to share ownership in it. If you're the only owner, you only get half the protection you signed up for—your personal liabilities may be protected from your business liabilities, but the reverse is not true.

To wrap up this chapter, let's answer the question we posed near the beginning: which is better for you, the corporation or the LLC? Because in most cases you can choose your taxation method, regardless of whether you're an LLC or a corporation, that no longer plays as big of a role in our decision-making as it once did.[51] It mostly comes down to protection, then. And because LLCs are more flexible and easier to manage, but provide the same liability protections as a corporation, if you're a small business owner, chances are it makes more sense to use an LLC.

---

[48] *In re Albright*, 291 B.R. 538 (D. Colo. 2003).
[49] Legalnature.com. "Asset Protection: The Corporate Veil and Charging Orders," available at https://www.legalnature.com/guides/asset-protection-the-corporate-veil-and-charging-orders, last accessed April 20, 2023.
[50] NRS 78.746. Elvis-themed weddings and charging order protection to corporations. Perhaps that's what attracted me to Las Vegas.
[51] There are certain situations where not all tax elections are available, so this is still important to look at when setting up your business.

CHAPTER 10

Maintaining Your LLC

Now that you've set up your medical practice as an LLC, you're protected, right? I mean, it's in the name: *limited liability* company. You've created separateness, and separateness means protection.

Unfortunately, nothing in the law is that cut and dried.

The reality is, setting up your LLC is just the first step. But like anything worth having, the LLC requires maintenance and care. We've got to show on an ongoing basis that your LLC is separate from you personally and from your other LLCs.

The two major advantages of setting up an LLC are liability protection—as we've just discussed—and tax savings—which we'll cover in Part III. There are rules for both, and unfortunately, although you are expected to follow them (and there are potential consequences if you don't), you probably have never been taught what you need to know.[1]

That's what this chapter is for.

Before I get into what you need to do to properly maintain your LLC, let's do a reality check. As you read through this chapter, you will more than likely realize that you've not been following the rules. You've been running your business all wrong. I don't want that to scare you. Is it important to do it right? Yes. Will it be detrimental to you if you don't? Perhaps (and hopefully) not.

---

[1] All those years at school and you still didn't learn this essential business information!

It's possible that from a legal perspective, you run your business all wrong, break all the rules of maintenance and violate all sorts of tax codes and never face any negative consequences.

For the most part, the rules for liability I teach you only matter if you're facing a claim or lawsuit, and the rules regarding taxes only matter if you get audited.

But then isn't that true of any protection? If you never get pulled over and never cause a crash, then it won't ever have mattered that you didn't have car insurance.

If you never lock your doors at night, it won't matter as long as no one ever tries to break in.

Don't have an umbrella? As long as it doesn't rain, you're as well off as everyone else.

Never get sued by a patient? Then whether your assets are separate is a moot point.

If you are someone who set up their LLC but then used it completely wrong, don't be too hard on yourself. You're in good company, though hopefully that doesn't give you a sense of complacence. There is still time to course correct.

If you don't want to follow the rules, well, that's okay, too. If you're prepared to accept the consequences. If you don't follow the rules for asset protection, there will be no protection. You might as well not have set up an LLC in the first place. All those annual fees you pay to the secretary of state? The extra money going to your CPA to file your business taxes every year? All wasted. But if your office manager breaches patient confidentiality and the patient comes after you, you're in trouble.

If you don't follow the rules for taxes, the consequences are steeper. You'll have to pay the taxes you owe, plus interest and penalties, and in some cases what you've done could be a crime.

My recommendation: although the risk is low, the stakes are high; so learn what you need to do and do it!

Alter Ego: A Question of Separateness

To understand what is required to maintain your health care LLC, you need to understand the legal doctrine of alter ego.

Let's go back to that Nevada LLC statute: "... no person other than the limited-liability company is individually liable for a debt or liability of the limited-liability company *unless the person acts as the alter ego of the limited-liability company.*"[2]

In other words, as long as you aren't the alter ego of your company, you won't be personally liable for your company's debts, and vice versa. So maintaining your LLC is really just a matter of not being its alter ego.

An alter ego is just an alternate version of the same person, right? Clark Kent's alter ego is Superman, Dr. Jekyll transformed into Mr. Hyde, and Bruce Wayne and Batman are one and the same. The alter ego is the person beneath the mask (or without the glasses, as it were).[3] They are the same person with two different identities. The outside world may not know it, but if one were to investigate, we'd see patterns: Bruce Wayne and Batman are never in the same place at the same time. Bruce Wayne is always tired during the day, and often has bruises. They have the same cleft chin and strong jawline. And as we get closer, if we're able to remove Batman's mask, the truth is revealed.

Now all that damage Batman did to the city while he was meting out vigilante justice? We can send Bruce Wayne the bill because they are alter egos of one another: they're the same person.

An LLC (or other business entity) is similar, but with some important differences. You can set up an LLC and be the only owner, have access to all the bank accounts, answer the phone and sign checks on its behalf, but the law says you are two separate people. No matter what Batman does, he's still just Bruce Wayne with a mask on, but you can set up an entity that for all intents and purposes, is a new person.

So alter ego is really a measure of *separateness*. If you are separate from your entity, you're not its alter ego, and the liability shield persists. If you are the alter ego, there is not sufficient separateness, and the liability protection fails. That liability failure is what we call piercing the corporate veil. Piercing the corporate veil is the natural consequence of a finding of alter ego.

---

[2] NRS 86.376 (emphasis added). This is Nevada's statute, but every state (to my knowledge) has an equivalent, whether born from statute or case law.

[3] As bad as Superman's disguise is, at least he changed his face with a new hairstyle and glasses. Remember He-Man? The only difference between him and Prince Adam was that He-Man wore fewer clothes and had a sword (though Prince Adam pulled the sword from somewhere before he held it aloft to become the most powerful man in the universe). They even both had the same blond bob and bangs. He-Man could have at least put his hair into a ponytail or changed his voice.

And although we think of LLCs as protecting us, alter ego is an important protection against the misuse of entities. To separate those who set up the entity as a front, and those who are using them legitimately. Indeed, "[a]s recognized by courts across the country, LLCs provide the same sort of possibilities for abuse as corporations, and creditors of LLCs need the same ability to pierce the LLCs' veil when such abuse exists."[4]

That raises the question, what standards does the law set to measure separateness? Or in other words, what are the factors a court considers when a claim for alter ego is brought?

We'll use Nevada's standard as a template, because that's the one I've litigated, but the factors will likely be very similar in your state.[5] Nevada has written the standard right into its statute:

A person acts as the alter ego of a limited-liability company only if:

(a) The limited-liability company is influenced and governed by the person;

(b) There is such unity of interest and ownership that the limited-liability company and the person are inseparable from each other; and

(c) Adherence to the notion of the limited-liability company being an entity separate from the person would sanction fraud or promote manifest injustice.[6]

Notice how the idea of separateness is threaded through all the base requirements. All the alter-ego statute is trying to measure is how separate you are from your business!

As helpful as it is to reduce the legal concept of alter ego into a word you understand, these factors are still rather general, and dare I say, vague. We need to drill down further. Luckily, Nevada courts have provided additional guidance as to what constitutes separateness

---

[4] *Gardner on Behalf of L.G. v. Eighth Jud. Dist. Ct. in & for Cnty. of Clark*, 133 Nev. 730, 736, 405 P.3d 651, 656 (2017).
[5] You can see a sampling of what other states require in this article put together by the Legal Information Institute at Cornell University: "Piercing the Corporate Veil," available at https://www.law.cornell.edu/wex/piercing_the_corporate_veil, last accessed April 18, 2023.
[6] NRS 86.376.

versus where a company and its owner are alter egos of one another. Here are a few:[7]

- Are funds commingled?
- Is the entity undercapitalized?
- Is there an unauthorized diversion of funds?
- Are the business assets treated as the individual's?
- Is there a failure to observe corporate formalities?

In my last trial before putting up my litigator hat and starting to work on behalf of doctors, both parties in the case were lawyers.[8]

An Ohio lawyer had done work for a Nevada lawyer in Ohio, and the Nevada lawyer did not pay him. The Ohio lawyer obtained a judgment in Ohio against the Nevada lawyer. However, because the Nevada lawyer's assets were all in Nevada, the Ohio lawyer needed to domesticate the judgment in Nevada (basically just have a Nevada court issue a twin judgment effective in Nevada).

The Ohio lawyer hired me for that purpose. We soon discovered that our Nevada judgment against the Nevada attorney was ineffective because the Nevada attorney had transferred all his assets into several entities. For that reason, we sued the Nevada attorney and all his entities for alter ego, and our purpose was to prove that he had not maintained the appropriate separateness between himself and his entities and between his entities and each other. We asked the court to issue a finding of alter ego and allow us to pierce the corporate veil, using assets of the various entities to satisfy the judgment we had against the Nevada lawyer.

What follows are segments of the actual transcripts of the depositions I took of the Nevada lawyer, David Fishman, and his partner, Constance Finnerman:[9]

David Fishman:

Q: Did Goldy [a Family Limited Partnership] ever file taxes?

---

[7] *LFC Mktg. Grp., Inc. v. Loomis*, 116 Nev. 896, 905, 8 P.3d 841, 847 (2000).

[8] *Folk v. Fishman, et al.*, A-16-733112. You'd think lawyers spend enough time in court that they wouldn't be starting their own lawsuits.

[9] One disadvantage of being sued is that all your private business now becomes part of the public record and can easily and legally become fodder for a story in a book that is part object lesson, part cautionary tale. David Fishman, if you're reading this, thanks for all the memories!

A: No.
Q: Did it have an operating agreement?
A: No.
Q: Did you establish bylaws for Goldy?
A: No.
Q: Did you hold any meetings?
A: No.
Q: Did you open a bank account?
A: No.
Q: Did you keep books of financial transactions?"
A: No.[10]

Q: Was Goldy ever capitalized?
A: No.[11]

Q: Okay. Did David Jane, LLC, operate at a profit?
A: Probably not.
Q: So it operated at a loss?
A: Probably so.[12]

Constance Finnerman:

Q: Okay. All three of these properties ... were all transferred into the trust?
A: Yes.
Q: But you're not sure why they were transferred?
A: Right.
Q: Okay. Do you remember signing papers making the transfer?
A: Yes.
Q: Okay. I'm going to pull these papers out. Let's do this one first.
A: I know why they were put in the trust to protect his grandchildren [sic].[13]

In addition to this testimony, there was evidence that the businesses and the trusts all used the same address, same fax number, same everything. Mr. Fishman was indiscriminate when it came to

---

[10] Goldy Dep. at 19:12–24.
[11] Goldy Dep. at 20:10–11.
[12] David Jane Dep. at 45:20–24.
[13] Finnerman Dep. at 17:16–18:4.

which company would pay the bills, so it wasn't unusual for a bill to an LLC to be paid by the corporation or vice versa.

We prevailed at trial, and the court expanded the judgment we had against David Fishman the individual. We could now use any assets belonging to any of his entities to satisfy that judgment.

David Fishman didn't keep his entities separate, so the court didn't keep the liabilities separate. And that's how it works for you, too. Separateness means liability protection.

CHAPTER 11

Business Ownership Best Practices

Now that you know what you know about the risks inherent with not maintaining separateness for each of your business entities, let's look at what specific steps you can take in your business to make sure you're never at risk of losing that liability protection through a veil-piercing lawsuit.

Like many other things in the law, every state has its own approach to setting up and maintaining a business entity. In Florida, for example, an LLC is not required to have an operating agreement.[1] Delaware and Nevada do not require corporations to keep minutes for their annual meetings.[2] Idaho does not require any fee to renew the LLC every year.[3]

Complying with state laws is obviously important, but just because your state doesn't require something to keep your LLC in good standing does not mean it's not a good idea, for liability reasons,[4] to

---

[1] Wong, B. "Florida LLC Operating Agreement (2023 Guide)," *Forbes.com*, February 1, 2023, available at https://www.forbes.com/advisor/business/florida-operating-agreement-llc, last accessed April 14, 2023.

[2] Akalp, "Do You Need Annual Meeting Minutes for Corporations and LLCs?" N. CorpNet.com, December 29, 2022, available at https://www.corpnet.com/blog/do-you-need-annual-meeting-minutes-for-corporations-and-llcs, last accessed April 14, 2023.

[3] Steingold, D.M. "Idaho LLC Annual Filing Requirements," Nolo.com, available at https://www.nolo.com/legal-encyclopedia/annual-report-tax-filing-requirements-idaho-llcs.html, last accessed April 14, 2023.

[4] I can't help but smile as I use that now hackneyed phrase. But I'm a lawyer, and I actually know what it means, I promise!

do everything you can to show that you're treating your business *separately* from yourself.

As an individual, you don't have to have an operating agreement. You don't have to file to renew every year. So everything you do for your business to show that it's separate and distinct from you, and that you are treating it as such, will be to your benefit if the separateness of your business is ever tested. To that end, here are some best practices for the observance of corporate formalities if your business is an LLC:

- Learn and comply with all the requirements of setting up your entity correctly. In most states, this will include at a minimum:
    o Registering the name of your business
    o Identifying a registered agent in the state authorized to accept legal service for the entity
    o Obtaining a federal tax ID number
    o Obtaining a business license
    o Submitting your articles of organization

- Ensure that your entity remains in good standing with your state. Different states have different requirements, but generally, that will require an annual report with a filing fee (sometimes called a "franchise tax"), and notifying the state of any changes in the interim to anything it has on file for you, including your registered agent and anything in the annual report.

- If you are doing business with a name different from your official entity name (commonly called a "DBA," "assumed name," or "fictitious firm name"), you'll want to register the fictitious firm name.

- Draft an operating agreement specific for your business. At a minimum, the operating agreement should include the following:
    o Identify the owners (members) of the LLC
    o Specify percentage ownership of each member
    o Enumerate the member contributions to the business
    o Establish procedure for distribution of profits

- o Establish procedure for transfer of ownership interests
- o Establish voting requirements and procedures (e.g., establish what decisions require unanimity versus majority vote)
- o Identify the manager(s) of the business
- o Record your first business meeting

- Follow the operating agreement in the operations of your business. If you want to do business contrary to the provisions of the operating agreement, amend the operating agreement so the two are always in accord.

- Set up a separate bank account for your entity. Keep your books clean, accurate, and separate from the bookkeeping of any other entity and your personal finances.

- If you are going to use a credit card for business purchases, open a business credit card using the name of your business. Do not open a personal credit card for business expenses, even if you use that one card exclusively for business purposes (even if you do get an extra 0.05% in credit card rewards!).

- Any business contracts should have your business as a party, not you. If your business is leasing space, it's the business on the contract, not you individually (though you may sign as a representative of the business, and the landlord may require a personal guarantee if your business has not established enough creditworthiness). Contracts with your clients and employees should be with the business, not with you individually.

- Invoices should be issued with the name and address of the business. Payment instructions should direct clients to pay the business, not you individually. (Never ever!)

- Hold meetings at least annually, plus any time the business makes a major decision. Keep minutes of those meetings, including who attended, what was discussed, and what was decided. Keep records of your minutes with your corporate books.

- Keep your entity properly capitalized. Make sure it has enough money to pay its bills. If you need to contribute personal money to the business to keep it capitalized, do so, and make sure it is logged on the books as a contribution. If you need to open a line of credit, do so in the name of the business, but don't risk overleveraging with an abnormally high debt-to-equity ratio. Do not pay distributions to yourself if the business is not in a suitable financial position.

- Have the business comply with all tax requirements, including timely issuance of W2s and 1099s; undertake federal and state income reporting; and make payment of other governmental taxes like sales taxes, use taxes, modified business taxes, and other local taxes.

- Obtain proper insurance, including, where applicable, errors and omissions, general liability, natural disaster, workers' compensation, and unemployment insurance.

- Limit business uses of personal property, and vice versa, but where it does occur, create a contract between you and your business that includes terms of use and payment. And then actually pay for its use.

- If you work for your business (most of us small business owners do), pay yourself a reasonable salary first,[5] then pay yourself a distribution if there are profits left in the business[6] (more on this at the end of the chapter).

These are best practices for an LLC. If your medical practice is a corporation, the formalities required are much stricter. Depending on

---

[5] What is a reasonable salary depends on what field you are in and where you live (you should be making something comparable to other people in your field in your area), and how many hours you work. Other factors, including how much education and training you have, how well you pay other employees, and what your duties and responsibilities are also come into play.

[6] This is more of a tax issue than any corporate formalities, but it's still a business-owner best practice.

your state, you may be required to hold meetings more often, you may have to appoint a board, establish bylaws, etc.

To help illustrate these bullet points, which you may well have (very understandably) skimmed past, let me give you some specific examples.

Personal Use of Company Assets and Vice Versa

I have a friend who is a dentist, and in his office, he has some sophisticated equipment that, outside of the office, I would call fun toys. For example, he has a high-resolution resin 3D printer that he uses for crown and bridge models. His business purchased the equipment, and his business uses the equipment for business purposes. It's a valid and legitimate business expense.

However, my friend also has fun with it. He printed a full-size Mandalorian helmet for his son. I didn't ask for details (no one wants their attorney friends taking their deposition during a social gathering), but let's assume when he used the business printer to build the helmet, he powered the machine using electricity paid for by the business and used resin the business had purchased.

Admittedly, as far as unauthorized diversion of business assets go, this is pretty benign and probably isn't going to be the silver bullet in a veil-piercing attempt from one of his creditors.

It could, however, be another nail in the coffin in an alter-ego case.

Assuming these facts are true (remember, I am making some assumptions here for my example), what could he have done differently?

The most obvious answer is not using the 3D printer at all for personal purposes. This is the safest approach, but there should be some benefits of owning a state-of-the-art, much-better-than-the-hobby-model-your-neighbor-has 3D printer, right?

The answer is simple: treat it like it is someone else's business. There are businesses out there that will 3D print for you. Why couldn't his?

As long as it is not contrary to anything in his operating agreement, he could draw up a simple contract where the dental practice allows him use of the 3D printer. There would have to be consideration, of course, so he'd have to pay the business for use of the printer, and that price would, at a minimum, have to cover the cost to the business.

You may think it's a little overboard to create a contract for something as insignificant as the use of $3 in resin and $0.15 in electricity, and perhaps you're right. But the more significant the business equipment, and the more frequent the use, the more important it's going to be to document the separateness with an arm's length agreement between you and your business. You can probably get away with a few prints here and there (but to be safe, have the business invoice you for its use!), but I wouldn't start regularly using your X-ray machine to analyze the composition of your coin or jewelry collection.[7]

Perhaps a better example is the business use associated with your personal vehicle, cell phone, and home office. Here, not only does it make sense from an alter-ego perspective to have an agreement that your business pay you for its use of your personal belongings, but it makes good tax sense, too. Doing it this way, not only do you legitimize the transaction for asset-protection purposes, but you can also legally transfer money from your business to you in a way that is not reportable as income, and therefore not taxable.[8]

Two Businesses Sharing Office Space, Employees, or Both

Suppose you own a small family medical practice. You purchase the building you operate out of, and you have more space than you need for your practice. Someone suggests that you open a med spa. After doing your due diligence, you agree that having the med spa share

---

[7] Confident that there must be some use of X-ray machines beyond just seeing inside a body, I asked Chatbot GPT 4, and the AI came up with a list of nonmedical uses for an X-ray that Google could not: "One such application is X-ray fluorescence (XRF) analysis, which is a non-destructive way to analyze the elemental composition of materials. XRF analysis can be used in various fields, including art conservation, archaeology, and geology. Hobbyists may also use XRF analysis to analyze the composition of coins, jewelry, and other objects.

"Another application of X-ray machines that may be of interest to hobbyists is radiography, which is the use of X-rays to create images of objects or materials. Radiography can be used in a variety of fields, such as engineering, aerospace, and manufacturing, to inspect the quality and integrity of materials and components."

[8] *See, e.g.,* IRS Publication 587, "Business Use of Your Home," available at https://www.irs.gov/pub/irs-pdf/p587.pdf, last accessed April 14, 2023; 26 CFR § 1.62–2. If your use of these items is more than half for business, it might make more sense for your business to purchase the vehicle or cell phone, get a deduction (and in some cases a tax credit) for the purchase, and then adjust at tax time the percentage of personal use of those items.

space with your family practice will be much more profitable than trying to grow your practice or rent out the space to a new tenant.

You've decided, then, to move forward with the med spa. How are you going to want to structure your businesses?

You already have an LLC set up for your family practice, so you're good there. But what about the building you're in? How should you own that? And the med spa? Should it operate under the same LLC as your family practice?

Let's take these questions one at a time. As more questions arise, we'll answer them, too.

The Commercial Building

If you own real estate, whether it be your primary residence or a commercial or residential investment property, you have several choices when it comes to ownership.

For investment properties, especially commercial ones, I always recommend having an LLC own it. Remember, the purpose of setting up an LLC is to create a legal separation. If you own the building in your name, then any liability that the building incurs implicates your personal assets, and any personal liabilities implicate the building. You don't want that.

But you also don't want to put it in the same LLC that owns and operates your family practice for the same reason: if someone gets hurt from some physical feature of the building (what we call premises liability), you don't want that X-ray machine or laser to be foreclosed on in satisfaction of someone's judgment.

The best practice for your commercial building is to put it in its own LLC—separate from everything else. If someone gets hurt in the building, then they're limited to taking the assets that the LLC owns, which will be limited to the building itself and a small bank account used to collect rents and pay the mortgage and other expenses. Just as important, if you incur personal liability, you don't risk losing the building your practice is operating out of.

But remember, creating the LLC and transferring ownership is only the beginning. You must maintain your LLC, too. In this case, that is going to include having a written lease between your commercial building LLC and any of its tenants, including the family practice LLC. Every month, your family practice is going to pay your commercial building rent. The commercial building is going to use that to pay the mortgage, if any, building repairs, tenant turnover costs, etc. Any left-over money can be paid to you as the property manager as a salary and to you the owner as a distribution.[9]

In other words, it's going to look just like any other landlord-tenant relationship. And that's the trick of separateness: even though you own both, you have to treat them like you don't.

The Medical Spa

When setting up your med spa, you have options. You could run the med spa through the same LLC as your family practice. If you do that, there is no separation between the med spa assets and liabilities and the family practice assets and liabilities. Perhaps that doesn't concern you because you have good insurance and are counting on your first line of defense to work should anything go wrong. That's your choice to make.

The better approach, in my opinion, would be to create a separate LLC. There is no reason to assume undue risk! Plus, if you have a partner in one but not the other, or you have different partners for both, it's going to be a must.

A little side note about this: Because you could feasibly separate every part of your business, you could maximize your liability protection, but it would come at a high administrative cost. For example, a dentist could set up five LLCs: one to do cleanings, one for consultations, one for cavities, one for crowns, and one for more major dental work like extractions or root canals.

In that scenario, if a patient needed a cleaning, a cavity filled, and a crown replaced, she would have to sign three contracts, pay three different times, and behind the scenes, each entity would have to track the work separately, bill each other for shared equipment (or own separate equipment), etc. You can imagine how much of a nightmare that would become.[10] The costs would outweigh the benefits.

But in a scenario where there is a clear break, like between a family practice and a med spa, the overlap isn't as high, and therefore neither is the cost. You'll have to do your own cost-benefit analysis, but I daresay in most cases it makes sense.

Here's how it works: You are going to set up an LLC in your state and get a federal EIN for it. With the organizing documents, EIN, and

---

[9] We'll discuss more later how to determine how much you pay yourself in a salary versus a distribution.
[10] I wouldn't want to suggest there's already a lot of paperwork when I go to get my teeth cleaned ... but there's certainly quite a few forms to sign. Mind, I can't talk, I'm a lawyer. I probably told you to have all those forms.

operating agreement, you go to the bank and open a business bank account. You'll fund the account either with your personal money (capital you contribute to your business is tax-deductible) or with a loan.

Now that your med spa LLC is established, you're going to set up the relationships. If there are clear divisions in the commercial building (i.e., separate units), then the med spa will contract directly with your commercial business for the lease. Suppose it isn't a separate unit, but rather separate patient rooms in one large unit. In that instance, you'll sublease part of the family practice's space and contract with the family practice instead (and you'll get the commercial building LLC to sign off on the sublease, which is probably required in the lease between it and the family practice).

If it's a sublease, you'll calculate the amount of rent based on the percentage of the unit used. For example, if there are ten equal-sized patient rooms and three common rooms that both businesses will use (like the reception area, break room, and storage), and the med spa will use four of the ten patient rooms. In that case, you'll allocate costs for the common rooms and split those costs, then add that to 40% of the remaining rent for the four rooms being used. The med spa will pay the family practice, and the family practice will pay the commercial building. Just like would happen if you didn't own all three.

What about employees? Shared inventory, disposables, and equipment? Again, we're going to simulate a scenario where all owners are separate.

If you want to share a receptionist, for example, and they answer line one for the family practice and line two for the med spa, and can set appointments for either, then both businesses are going to have to contribute to their salary.

In that scenario, they will work for one of the businesses, and that business will invoice the other for their services. Or you could hire a reception company that employs the receptionist and invoices your two businesses separately, which they might do by billing you per call handled to your respective lines.

I do not recommend sharing phone numbers even if both numbers ring to the same phone or same receptionist service—you do not want your patients confusing the two businesses because if they don't look separate from the outside, a court may not treat them as separate when it comes to the alter-ego liability analysis. That very issue has come to bear in more than one of my cases. When two businesses share a phone number, they don't look like separate businesses.

You're also going to have signage for both companies and, if feasible, two doors that go from the waiting room—one with a sign for the med spa, and one for the family practice. The more separation you can create in your business practices, the more likely that separation will be recognized in a liability analysis.

You'll have to consider this idea of separateness with anything the two businesses share. If you only have one supply room, for example, how are you going to keep track of the use of disposable gloves, rags, and tongue depressors?

You could have one shelf for one business and one shelf for another. Your employees would have to be trained to only pull from the one shelf. And if the med spa has run out of gloves, but the family practice still has some, there should be a procedure that allows for the med spa to purchase gloves from the other.

Or you could keep all your inventory together but have each item logged separately. If the family practice purchases all the inventory for storage, it would then bill the med spa at the end of the month for everything the med spa takes from the storage room, as reflected in the logs. And of course, there is going to be some markup because legitimate businesses don't provide ongoing services for free.

These aren't the only options, but should serve as an example of the exercises you should undertake to ensure separateness, both between you your businesses and between your businesses themselves.

If it's not separate in your business, it won't be separate in court.

CHAPTER 12

The Series LLC

The LLC solved a big problem for small business owners: getting the benefit of limited liability without the cost of double taxation. And in the 46 years since its birth, the LLC has risen to become the most common type of business entity, by far.

The next step in the evolution of small business is the Series LLC, which takes the benefits of the LLC and makes them scalable without becoming unwieldy.

If you are a small business owner who has one medical practice, the traditional LLC is likely going to be perfect for you. You register it, keep the state renewals up to date, keep your books clean, hold your annual meetings, file taxes, and otherwise maintain the entity. You've got the liability protection, the tax benefits, and with some hard work and a little luck, a profitable business.

But what if you want to open a company to develop that cutting-edge medical device for your practice? And a pharmacy? And a health insurance brokerage? And a space tourism business?[1] You've got five businesses, and all that maintenance you have to do gets multiplied by five. Five renewal fees, five EIN numbers, five tax filings, five of everything.[2]

We can really highlight the benefits of the Series LLC with the example of real estate investing. And in my experience, real estate is

---

[1] OK, that's probably rarer than my cabinet-making/lawyer combination.
[2] Like having five kids, having five separate LLCs is a lot of hard work, but without the joy of witnessing five first smiles.

where medical professionals turn first when deciding where to invest their expendable income. For reasons explained in previous chapters (rule 1 of asset protection: keep assets separate from liabilities), if you have multiple investment properties, you do not want them all owned by the same LLC, and you especially don't want the titles to be in your name individually.

Many savvy real estate investors will create a separate LLC for each property. This provides both tax advantages and asset protection for each property, not only for the owner, but also property to property.

When each property is owned by a separate LLC, and you incur personal liability, your creditors cannot take your property (assuming your LLC is formed in a state with charging order protection that applies to you). Further, if one of your LLCs incurs liability (like if someone gets hurt at one of the properties), the judgment creditor cannot take your personal things, and it cannot take assets of any other property, either because the LLC they have a judgment against doesn't own any of those things.

Although having several LLCs does get you the benefits you want as a real estate investor, the more homes you purchase, the more unwieldy it gets. Every new property multiplies your administrative burden and cost.

Setting up a single Series LLC is not going to eliminate all added burden and expense, but it will offer some efficiency that you can't get with multiple LLCs without sacrificing any of the legal benefits.

Here is how a Series LLC works:[3]

When registering an LLC with Nevada, you do so like you normally would, except you indicate that the LLC is going to authorize the creation of one or more series.[4] The LLC operating agreement authorizes the creation of one or more series and declares that the debts, liabilities, obligations, and expenses of the series are enforceable against only that series, and voila!, your Series LLC is complete.[5] Now, whenever you want to create a new series, you adopt a resolution to do so (recorded in documented minutes of the Series LLC), name the series, draft an operating agreement for that series, and it's done. Typically, with a Series LLC, you'll use the name of the parent Series LLC and a subname for the series itself. So if you register

---

[3] Although different states have different rules and ideas for a Series LLC, all those states that have adopted them will have some similarities. I am most familiar with Nevada Series LLCs, so they will be the focus of this discussion.
[4] NRS 86.296(2).
[5] *Id.*

the LLC as "Red Hot Real Estate, LLC," your first series, series A, may be called "Red Hot Real Estate, LLC Series A," and the next one "Red Hot Real Estate, LLC Series B."

Alternatively, you could name each series based on what it does or owns. If you are setting up a separate series for each property you purchase, and you purchase a property on Maple Street, you may call the series that owns it "Red Hot Real Estate, LLC Series Maple." Legally, what you name it doesn't really matter, as long as each one is unique. From a practical stance, though, your naming convention could either make it easier or more confusing to keep them all straight. It's harder to remember that the Maple address was "Series F" than to remember it is "Series Maple," after all.

If you maintain "Series Maple" like you would any other LLC (treating this individual series as a separate entity), you've got all the protections of an additional LLC without having to register a new LLC with the state. In fact, you don't even file a new articles of organization with Nevada when you set up your new series in your Series LLC.[6]

You can now have a separate series for every property you own, but only have one entity to renew every year, and one entity that you have to pay a renewal fee for every year.

Those are the basics. If I were to describe the Series LLC in a nutshell, it would be like this: with a Series LLC you can get the asset protection of multiple LLCs without having to register and renew multiple LLCs.

That means, if you're a real estate investor, the more properties you have, the more efficient the Series LLC gets.

How Are Series LLCs Taxed?

For now, the Series LLC, and all the series created under it, are taxed as a single entity.[7] The tax efficiency that comes with a Series LLC is an added bonus.

---

[6] *Id.*

[7] Danao, M & Main, K. "What Is a Series LLC? Everything You Need to Know," August 18, 2022, Forbes Advisor, available at
https://www.forbes.com/advisor/business/what-is-series-llc, last accessed May 2, 2023.

Even if the IRS changes the rule and starts requiring each series to be taxed separately (which it has suggested might happen[8]), you won't be any worse off than if you had separate LLCs. You won't be paying any more in taxes (like LLCs, these are pass-through entities), and there won't be additional work over having several LLCs.

What If I Live in a State That Doesn't Have Its Own Version of a Series LLC?

Currently, 18 states and the District of Columbia (and counting) have some version of the Series LLC.[9] But what if you live in a state that hasn't adopted it yet? Are you out of luck? Not at all.

The first thing you need to know is that you will have to register your Series LLC in the state you're doing business in (same as you have to do if it were any other kind of business entity). In simple terms, you are notifying the state that you are doing business inside its borders. You have to provide, usually to the secretary of state, the name and origin state of your entity, and you have to appoint someone within the state's borders, called a registered agent, to accept official notices and legal service on behalf of the entity.

This requirement is meant to protect the consumers in that state doing business with your entity. Suppose someone has a claim against the entity. Instead of trying to figure out what state it's based in and tracking down someone related to the entity, they just have to look you up in their state, and deliver their notice to the registered agent. The agent's job it is to forward those notices to you.

If you live in the state you're doing business in, you can serve as the registered agent (if you're willing to post your address publicly), or you can hire a professional agent, which normally costs somewhere between $50 and $200 per year.

Now that you're officially registered, what if something happens? Will your state recognize the entity created in another state?

The United States Constitution has something to say about that: "Full Faith and Credit shall be given in each State to the public Acts,

---

[8] IRS.gov, "Notice of Proposed Rulemaking Series LLCs and Cell Companies," November 8, 2010, REG-119921-09, available at https://www.irs.gov/irb/2010-45_IRB#REG-119921-09, last accessed May 2, 2023.

[9] Those states are Alabama, Arkansas, Delaware, Illinois, Indiana, Iowa, Kansas, Missouri, Montana, Nevada, North Dakota, Oklahoma, Puerto Rico, Tennessee, Texas, Utah, Virginia, Washington, D.C., and Wyoming. *Id.*

Records, and judicial Proceedings of every other State."[10] That means that every state has to recognize and give "full faith and credit" to the laws of other states.

So in California, where the legislature has not established their own version of the Series LLC, a court cannot just disregard a Series LLC that has been formed lawfully in another state.

That's not to say that there wouldn't or couldn't be complications, though. Under conflict of laws principals, if the laws of a sister state, which by the Constitution must be given full faith and credit, conflict with the laws of the forum state (the state you're in), there is a procedure for resolving that conflict.

Suppose California were to create a law on its books that said "all property in this state must be owned by any individual living anywhere or an LLC formed in this state."[11] Further suppose that the court was faced with a case where an LLC (including a Series LLC) from Nevada was found to have purchased property under a Nevada state law that said "a limited liability company formed in this state has the same rights and legal authority as any individual."

Here we would have a conflict of laws because Nevada imbues its LLCs with human-like rights, and California distinguishes between out-of-state LLCs and individuals. And although California is required to give full faith and credit to Nevada laws, if a case cannot be resolved in a way that both laws are followed, it must engage in a conflict-of-laws analysis to determine which state laws will apply. "When it is demanded in the domestic forum that the operation of those laws be supplanted by the statute of another state, that forum is not bound, apart from the full faith and credit clause, to yield to the demand, and the law of neither can, by its own force, determine the choice of law for the other."[12]

An education on conflict-of-laws principles is beyond the scope of this book[13], but it turns out we don't really have to go there because those states who do not have a mechanism for creating a Series LLC within their borders tend to like the Series LLCs created in other states and doing business in their own.

I will use California as an example because that's the state I hear referenced most (read: pretty much the only state mentioned) when

---

[10] U.S. Const. Art. IV § 1.
[11] That could very well be unconstitutional on other grounds, but let's run with it for our purposes anyway.
[12] *Pink v. A. A. A. Highway Express, Inc.*, 314 U.S. 201, 209 (U.S. 1941).
[13] I bet you're relieved about that.

people express concerns about the Series LLC. They have heard, after doing some preliminary research (i.e., read a blog article or two), that California "doesn't recognize Series LLCs and would probably disregard them."

You don't have to look far to find this kind of thinking, and it's almost always in reference to California:

- "The biggest problem with Series LLCs is that many states (including California) don't have series legislation and may choose to ignore the laws of the state where the series was created."[14]

- "There is currently little state legislation leading to uncertainty as to how the Series LLC would be treated by the courts."[15]

- "California's state legislature has not yet formally allowed for the creation of a Series LLC. Members/managers of foreign Series LLCs run the risk of being denied the separate liability protection that Series LLCs are designed to provide in their home states because the law on Series LLCs operating California is sparse."[16]

I suspect that rather than doing independent research to arrive at conclusions, these blog authors (none of whom, interestingly enough, attached their names to the articles), did some cursory internet research, came across some other blogs, and regurgitated the main message: California's legislature is silent on the issue, so there is uncertainty as to how it would be treated in court.

I have little doubt that these conclusions came from people who have never argued in court.

Rather than get my legal advice from anonymously written blogs boasting acumen of the law but lacking any legal authority, I decided,

---

[14] Corporate Direct, "The Four Dangers of Series LLCs," available at https://corporatedirect.com/real-estate/series-llcs-where-angels-fear-to-tread, last accessed May 2, 2023.
[15] CSULB, "New Business Structures: Series LLC," April 2, 2023, available at https://www.csulb.edu/college-of-business/legal-resource-center/article/new-business-structures-series-llc, last accessed May 2, 2023.
[16] Theta Law Firm, "How to Operate a Series LLC in California," available at http://thetafirm.com/articles/how_to_operate_series_LLC_in_CA.html, last accessed May 2, 2023.

after hearing several times about the risks of using a Nevada Series LLC in California, to do my own research.

And so, I looked up and read *every single* California case mentioning the term "Series LLC." These mentions included everything from oblique references to in-depth discussions.

Turns out, California does not just tolerate the Series LLC; it loves it.

I did not find a single negative reference to the Series LLC. Those cases that discussed it with any depth spoke positively of the entity.

In a pair of cases involving insurance companies,[17] a California federal court had to determine whether a Series LLC had the authority to sue on behalf of the subseries created within it. California disagreed with other courts in other states and took the position that, yes, the parent Series LLC could sue on behalf of the subseries. This is significant because it represents California taking a position where it affirmatively recognizes a Series LLC created in other states and does so favorably.

In a case involving a wellness center, California uses language to suggest that an LLC and a series in a Series LLC are functionally similar.[18]

In another case, one of the issues hinged on whether the Series LLC had been created before or after a transaction, suggesting that if it had been created before, the issue would be resolved favorably for the plaintiff, but if it had been backdated to be created fraudulently, it wouldn't.[19] The court did not find any fraud and didn't ever question the legitimacy of the Series LLC; it treated it as though it were an old friend.[20]

Another pair of cases merely mentions the Series LLC but doesn't really discuss it.[21] This is significant because California is acting like the Series LLC is no big deal. Nowhere does it say anything like

---

[17] *MAO-MSO Recovery II, LLC v. Mercury Gen.*, No. CV1702525ABAJWX, 2021 WL 6102913, at *4 (C.D. Cal. Nov. 29, 2021); *MSP Recovery Claims, Series LLC v. Farmers Ins. Exch.*, No. 217CV02522CASPLAX, 2018 WL 5086623, at *14 (C.D. Cal. Aug. 13, 2018).

[18] *N. Am. Wellness Ctr., LLC v. Holmes*, No. 3:14-CV-2584-CAB-BGS, 2015 WL 1291372, at *2 (S.D. Cal. Mar. 23, 2015).

[19] *Wagner v. Spire Vision LLC*, No. C 13-04952 WHA, 2015 WL 876514, at *5 (N.D. Cal. Feb. 27, 2015).

[20] *Id.*

[21] *Miranda v. Gaslamp Tavern Oceanview Series, LLC*, No. G043982, 2012 WL 1385491, at *1 (Cal. Ct. App. Apr. 23, 2012); *Gilmore Bank v. Dalrymple*, No. G047902, 2014 WL 2763658, at *2 (Cal. Ct. App. June 18, 2014).

"the Series LLC is not recognized in California ..." When the Series LLC comes up in front of the court, they aren't taking a sidebar to explain the Series LLC or excuse its existence. They just treat it like any other entity.

In one case, the court does a corporate veil-piercing analysis and handles series in a Series LLC just like any other set of separate entities and suggests that overlapping ownership between the series is evidence of alter ego that could lead to piercing the corporate veil[22] (which is the case when comparing any other two entities). This is why we teach our clients to keep separate books and to make sure to observe corporate formalities in their separate series.

There are other California cases I found in my research that I haven't referenced here, but it's just more of the same: treating the Series LLC just like any other entity.

Perhaps the reason that California has embraced the entity from other states is that it's still collecting its pound of flesh. Indeed, although setting up a Series LLC will save you in renewal time and money in Nevada, you won't escape California's dreaded franchise tax. The Golden State charges $800 for each series doing business in its state.[23]

Although no one is going to get excited about that $800 fee, (1) it just goes to show how separate even California considers each series to be, and (2) you still aren't any worse off for this than you would be if you had separate LLCs (in other words, the efficiency benefit you get from the Series LLC is still there, but it doesn't extend to California franchise taxes).

Potential Downside of the Series LLC

The Series LLC is not for everyone. The more properties you own, or the more related businesses you want to run, the more sense it makes. Even so, because the Series LLC is still relatively new, when you have to do business with third parties, it can sometimes be a little extra work.

---

[22] *Jacobson v. Persolve, LLC*, No. 14-CV-00735-LHK, 2015 WL 2061712, at *4 (N.D. Cal. May 1, 2015).
[23] California Franchise Tax Board, "Series LLC," available at https://www.ftb.ca.gov/file/business/types/limited-liability-company/series-limited-liability-company.html, last accessed May 2, 2023. Californians can still be smiling about the beautiful climate and beaches though.

For example, setting up a bank account for a series is not going to be as straightforward as it is for an ordinary LLC. Although any bank will set one up for the Series LLC itself, it's a different story if you want to set up separate accounts for each series in the Series LLC. Some banks will have no problem. Others will do it if you register your series as a fictitious firm name, or DBA of the parent Series LLC[24] (they want to be able to look up your entity online, which they can't do with a Nevada series because the individual series aren't registered), and others won't do it under any circumstances.

I expect as the Series LLC gains more popularity, this will change, but for now, some are afraid of the unfamiliar.

I Have a Series LLC

When I speak to you about the Series LLC, I do so from personal experience. I have two Nevada Series LLCs—one for real estate and one for a franchise business I own. Let me walk you through my experience using them so you have an idea what they can be used for and what the day-to-day is like.

Real Estate Investing

As of the time of this writing, I own one investment property in Citrus Springs, Florida near the west coast about an hour and a half north of Tampa.[25]

In anticipation of this transaction, I created a Nevada Series LLC. Because I only have one property, any LLC would have worked just fine, but since I plan on purchasing more properties in the future, I created the series to give me room to grow without incurring extra annual costs for each entity.

Let's say the name of my Series LLC is Parry Properties, LLC. When I purchase another property, I will fill out schedule 1.1 in my operating agreement (a two-page form whose purpose is to create series within the Series LLC).

---

[24] This is not something you'll want to do. Registering it as a DBA is like announcing that the two businesses are the same, which is the exact opposite of what we're doing here.

[25] Purchasing this property was about the easiest thing I ever did. My firm has partnered up with a company that does plug-and-play real estate investing. They help you find the property, fund the purchase, and manage it. Easiest thing I've ever done. If you want me to introduce you, shoot me an email: zach@thefortunelawfirm.com.

That form names the series, lists its owner (which is, in most cases, going to be the parent series), and designates the manager.

The name of the series can be anything (as long as each series has a unique name). So if my second property is on 1.21 Gigawatt Street, then perhaps it makes sense to me to name the series 1.21 Gigawatt. If I do, then the full name of the series will be "Parry Properties, LLC series 1.21 Gigawatt."

Now all I need for my series to be official is an operating agreement. Once I have that, I can transfer property into the series.

To do that, I will use either a warranty deed or quitclaim deed[26] to transfer it from the grantor's name (mine) into the grantee's name (my series).

I send that deed to be recorded at the county recorder's office in the county where the property is located, following their procedures. I pay what is usually a nominal fee, and after a couple weeks, they'll send me the record-stamped document. Now my series owns the property!

If this is the first property I have purchased in that state, I will also notify the state that my Nevada series is doing business in their state. Each state has different procedures for that, but it usually consists of filing a one- or two-page document with the secretary of state (usually called a "foreign entity filing" or something akin to that), paying their fee (also usually nominal), and identifying a registered agent in that state.

The registered agent is someone who lives within the borders of the state (or an entity with a location in that state) who is appointed to receive official notices on behalf of that entity at a mailing address within the state and then forward it to you.

Now you just make sure the property management company (if you have one) and the tenant are entering contracts with your series, not with you, and rent payments are going into an account associated with the series (not your personal bank account). From there, you run the series like you would any other LLC.

Franchise Business

---

[26] Some states, like Tennessee, will tax you for the transfer if you use a warranty deed, but not if you use a quitclaim deed. Other states will tax you for the transfer unless there is unity in ownership, i.e., you owned it individually, and you are transferring it into an entity wholly owned by you. Other states, like Pennsylvania, will tax you on this type of transfer no matter what.

In 2022, my brother, Jacob, and I bought a waxing (hair removal) franchise that we planned to operate in the Las Vegas Valley. He opened his first location in Henderson (a Las Vegas suburb), and I opened mine on the opposite side of the valley in Las Vegas.

We wanted to run our businesses cooperatively, but separately, so we each set up a separate LLC. We also set up a third LLC that would perform the functions that the two waxing businesses had in common, like paying a manager who would manage the employees and inventory in both locations.

For the first several months, this was all we needed. Then we both decided to open a second location. Realizing that we were likely each going to be operating several locations, we set up a Series LLC that we co-own, which would be the entity from which we operated all future locations.

Inside the Series LLC, I set up a series for the purpose of owning and operating my second location, and although Jacob and I co-own the parent LLC, I own the series 100%. He did the same thing and set up a series specifically for his second location that he owns 100%.

Had we realized when we started that we would be growing into multiple locations, we would have set up the Series LLC to start instead of each setting up a separate LLC. Live and learn.

We are planning ahead for a third location each, and for those, we will also each set up a new series. At that point, our organizational structure will look like this:

LLC	Type	Location	Ownership	
Management LLC	LLC	No physical location	Zach:	50%
			Jacob:	50%
LLC 1	LLC	Northern Las Vegas	Zach:	100%
LLC 2	LLC	Henderson	Jacob:	100%
LLC 3	Series LLC	No physical location	Zach:	50%
			Jacob:	50%
LLC 3 Series 1	Series	Northwest Las Vegas	Zach:	100%
LLC 3 Series 2	Series	Southeast Las Vegas	Jacob:	100%
LLC 3 Series 3	Series	Central Las Vegas	Zach:	100%
LLC 3 Series 4	Series	Southwest Las Vegas	Jacob:	100%

Here, the LLC 1 and LLC 2 and the last four series are functionally identical: they each have operating agreements, they each have a separate employer identification number,[27] separate bank accounts, separate QuickBooks accounts, separate employees, etc.

My employees who work at more than one location have more than one employer and will clock their time based on where they are working. They also receive more than one paycheck.

Jacob and I have each hired a separate manager to manage our respective locations. The management LLC employs them, pays them on payday, and then invoices each of the locations (either the LLC or series that owns them) for a pro-rata share of the management. Each of these locations then pays the management LLC.

Now, no matter how many locations we open, we will only have four LLCs: the management LLC, the two original non-Series LLCs, and the one Series LLC. At some point in the future if we desire, we can transfer ownership of the first two locations from the LLCs to a new series, and we will only ever have two LLCs to maintain with the state.[28] We know many other franchise owners with multiple locations. Most of them have a single LLC that owns and operates all their locations. There is nothing illegal about that, and management of their businesses is simpler than ours. They only have one LLC employing everyone, only have one set of payroll to run, and don't have to issue invoices among locations.

However, if a client, employee, or guest exposes one location to liability, the assets of all of the franchisee's locations are potentially at risk.

When deciding how to move forward with your business—whether it's the sort of health-related businesses we discussed earlier or other business interests—you have to evaluate your own risk tolerance versus administrative burden and decide if the extra regular work of maintaining multiple LLCs or multiple series is worth the extra protection. For me, it is, particularly when a Series LLC affords me the protection of multiple LLCs with the renewal cost of only one.

---

[27] A series doesn't technically have to have its own EIN, but I am operating separate businesses within each series, and not just holding property, so I opted for separate EINs and separate bank accounts.

[28] We could do that now, but when you switch ownership of a business, on paper it looks like the business is new, so it could complicate future SBA loans if we can't show two years' history when we're looking to expand.

CHAPTER 13

The Asset Protection Trust

There are many different types of trusts, all of which are built slightly differently and have different purposes. Some can be changed at will. Some cannot. Some have tax advantages. Some do not. Some protect assets. And you guessed it, some do not.

Although we will talk about living trusts in chapters 16 and 18 in greater detail, they form a framework for understanding the asset protection trust, so we'll do a brief review of them now.

Living trusts have been around for hundreds of years,[1] the first one in America having been established in 1765 by the Lieutenant Governor of Virginia to ensure his family could get his assets without having to go through any lengthy court process.[2]

The person who establishes the trust (the trustor, settlor, or grantor) transfers their property into the trust and then gives the trust instructions to transfer it in turn to named beneficiaries at the trustor's death, thereby obviating the need for a court to determine what happens to the deceased's property.[3] The deceased, after all, has

---

[1] They were originally established in 15th century England as a way for noblemen from preventing the King from seizing their assets by virtue of accusations that would entitle the king to seize their property after death. The Law Offices of Jeffrey G. Marsocci, PLLC, "A Quick History of Revocable Living Trusts," available at https://livingtrustlawfirm.com/a-quick-history-of-revocable-living-trusts, last accessed August 22, 2023.

[2] *Id.*

[3] *Com. Bank, N.A. v. Bolander*, 44 Kan. App. 2d 1, 13, 239 P.3d 83, 91 (2007).

no property, only the trust does, and the trust is still "alive" and can dispose of its own property.

These types of "living" trusts are also revocable, meaning they can be changed during the trustor's lifetime.[4] However, once the trustor dies, the trust becomes irrevocable and can no longer be altered.[5]

This makes sense. When I determine when I am alive that I want Johnny to get my action figure collection and Maria to get the jewelry, and then I die, so too, do my desires, so my last expressed desire should be the one my heirs are bound to.

So if Maria wants some action figures after I die, she's not going to get it through any judicial process or petition to the trustee. She's going to have to wait until Johnny gets them and then try and convince him to let her have some.

But what about creditors? Let's suppose your trust directs all of your assets to be given to your only child. When you die, you also have a creditor who makes a claim against part of the proceeds of your estate. Your creditor wants to get paid before your child does on the basis that if you had lived longer, it would have been paid, and your estate would have been smaller when you died, so your child would have only gotten the remainder.

Does the trust have to pay the creditor's claims?

That's going to depend on a number of factors, like the state you're in. In Ohio, the creditor would be out of luck.[6] Kansas[7] and California[8] would allow the creditor to pursue the claim.

Perhaps because of this, trustors began creating trusts with "spendthrift" provisions. Now, we will explore spendthrift provisions and how they became the doorway to asset protection.

Spendthrift Provisions

A spendthrift provision is a clause in a trust that invokes a *"valid* restraint on the voluntary and involuntary transfer of the interest of the beneficiary."[9] That means the beneficiary cannot spend or borrow against trust funds (a voluntary transfer), nor can the

---

[4] *Tseng v. Tseng*, 271 Or. App. 657, 660, 352 P.3d 74, 76 (2015).
[5] *Ayers v. Mitchell*, 167 S.W.3d 924, 930 (Tex. App. 2005).
[6] *Schofield v. Cleveland Tr. Co.*, 135 Ohio St. 328, 333, 21 N.E.2d 119, 122 (1939).
[7] K.S.A. 58a–505(a)(3); *Bolander*, 44 Kan. App. at 13, 239 P.3d at 92.
[8] Cal. Prob. Code § 19001(a).
[9] *Matter of Frei Irrevocable Tr. Dated Oct. 29, 1996*, 133 Nev. 50, 54–55, 390 P.3d 646, 651 (2017) (citing NRS 166.020).

beneficiary's creditors access the trust assets (an involuntary transfer).[10]

Therefore, as a result of the spendthrift provision, neither the beneficiary nor the beneficiary's creditors may access the trust's assets or use any legal process to dispose of or pledge part of the trust income or estate.[11]

In some states, like Nevada, this protection explicitly strips courts of their power to issue orders around the protection:

> [A spendthrift trust beneficiary] shall have no power or capacity to make any disposition whatever of any of the income ... whether made upon the order or direction of any court or courts, whether of bankruptcy or otherwise; nor shall the interest of the beneficiary be subject to any process of attachment issued against the beneficiary, or to be taken in execution under any form of legal process directed against the beneficiary or against the trustee, or the trust estate, or any part of the income thereof, but the whole of the trust estate and the income of the trust estate shall go to and be applied by the trustee solely for the benefit of the beneficiary, free, clear, and discharged of and from any and all obligations of the beneficiary whatsoever and of all responsibility therefor.[12]

Such spendthrift provisions make it clear that the beneficiary of a trust cannot encumber or assign their interest in the trust estate.[13] The name suggests that it was originally designed to protect a young or foolish beneficiary from their own excessive habits as a "spendthrift" is "a person who spends improvidently or wastefully."[14]

Imagine a scenario where you realize your child will squander his inheritance if he receives it all at once. To protect him from his own excessive nature, you set up the trust to mete out his inheritance month by month. Instead of receiving it all now, he gets $2,500 per month until the trust assets are exhausted.

---

[10] McDonald, T, Newton, E, Graessle, J. "The State of Domestic Self-Settled Asset Protection Trusts," Autumn *Forensic Accounting and Special Investigations Thought Leadership*, Insights, (2019) at 14.

[11] *Frei*, 133 Nev. at 54–55, 390 P.3d at 651 (citing NRS 166.120(1)–(3)). *See also Klabacka v. Nelson*, 133 Nev. 164, 175, 394 P.3d 940, 949 (2017).

[12] NRS 166.120(3).

[13] *Cronquist v. Utah State Agr. Coll.*, 114 Utah 426, 430, 201 P.2d 280, 282 (1949).

[14] Merriam Webster's Dictionary, "Spendthrift," https://www.merriam-webster.com/dictionary/spendthrift.

Your son does the math and realizes over the next ten years, he'll get $300,000. He isn't happy with $2,500 per month, so he finds a willing buyer, and that buyer is willing to pay $100,000 now in exchange for $2,500 per month for 10 years.

It's a good deal for the buyer because he is spending $100,000 to get a guaranteed $300,000 over time.

And although it's not a great deal for your son, he prefers it. He'd rather have a smaller lump sum now than have a larger number trickle to him over ten years.

A spendthrift provision would prevent that from happening by making it clear that the beneficiary, your son, has no right to encumber or assign those future rights.

It would also prevent him from using the guaranteed payments to qualify for a loan so he can't just go purchase an expensive car on credit based on the promise of future payments coming from the trust.

And although there is certainly benefit from protecting your children from themselves, the spendthrift provision also protects them against creditors.

Suppose your son incurs medical bills he cannot pay. His creditor—the hospital—can use every legal means at its disposal to collect on the debt, but placing a lien on a trust with a spendthrift provision will not be one of them. Because the assets in the trust belong to the trust until distributed, and the trust did not incur the debt, the creditor has no right to trust assets.

Like everything else law-related, spendthrift provisions are going to be allowable to differing degrees in different states. But they can be a powerful tool to protect the assets of a trust from the creditors of its beneficiaries.

In this scenario, where the spendthrift provision kicks in only after death, when your revocable trust becomes irrevocable, its benefits during your life are limited.

You can, though, set up an irrevocable trust during your lifetime for the benefit of your family and then fund it during your lifetime with your assets (which means you permanently and "irrevocably" give up rights to those assets). This can have estate tax benefits, make it easier to qualify for government benefits, and protect assets.[15]

As an asset-protection device, though, an irrevocable trust set up for the benefit of someone else is hardly ideal because to protect those

---

[15] Kagan, J. "Irrevocable Trusts Explained: How They Work, Types, and Uses," September 9, 2022, *Investopedia*, available at https://www.investopedia.com/terms/i/irrevocabletrust.asp (last accessed August 22, 2023).

assets, it requires you to give them away. A creditor can't take something that isn't yours, after all.[16]

You could just as well protect your assets by giving them to charity or dumping wads of cash out of a ten-story window on a windy day. If you have to give it away to protect it, you might as well pay your creditor and keep what's left unless you were going to give it away anyway.[17]

However, what if you could create an irrevocable trust, including a spendthrift provision, thereby protecting the assets from the beneficiaries' creditors, but you made yourself the beneficiary, with allowances through which you could authorize the trust to transfer its assets back to you?

For most of history, this was not possible. The very idea of the trustor/grantor/settlor (creator) of the trust also being the beneficiary would have seemed absurd. Trusts, by their very nature, are for the benefit of other people.

That changed in 1997 when Alaska created the first self-settled spendthrift trust.

Self-Settled Trusts

When a trust is "self-settled," it means the settlor (its creator) is also the beneficiary.[18] A self-settled spendthrift trust is an irrevocable trust set up by and for the benefit of the same person to protect assets.

Historically, such protections were only available outside the United States, like in the Cayman Islands or Bermuda,[19] and were known as offshore asset protection trusts.

Alaska was the first state in the nation to introduce such a trust in the U.S. Its explicit purpose was to "find a way to stimulate economic development in Alaska" (presumably by encouraging people from

---

[16] Unless they were a creditor before you gave it away, in which case they may be able to void the transfer, clawing it back, based on principles of fraudulent conveyance. *See Finn v. All. Bank*, 838 N.W.2d 585, 597 (Minn. Ct. App. 2013), aff'd as modified, 860 N.W.2d 638 (Minn. 2015).

[17] Although giving away your money will prevent your creditor from getting it, it won't make the judgment go away, so if you get more money in the future, they could try to take that.

[18] TRUST, Black's Law Dictionary (11th ed. 2019); *De Prins v. Michaeles*, 486 Mass. 41, 45, 154 N.E.3d 921, 925–26 (2020).

[19] Veit, JM. "Self-Settled Spendthrift Trusts and the Alaska Trust Act: Has Alaska Moved Offshore?" 16 *Alaska L. Rev.* 269 (1999)

other states to pay professionals in Alaska to set up and maintain them) "and establish Alaska as a global financial center."[20]

For the first time, then, it became possible for an individual, without sending money offshore, to create a trust, name themselves as a beneficiary, transfer their funds to the trust where it presumably lay beyond the reach of a creditor, and then take the assets back via distribution.

This idea was (and in some cases still is) repugnant to some jurisdictions.

> The invalidity of self-settled spendthrift trusts [in Georgia] stems from the idea that no settlor ... should be permitted to put his own assets in a trust, of which he is the sole beneficiary, and shield those assets with a spendthrift clause, because to do so is merely shifting the settlor's assets from one pocket to another, in an attempt to avoid creditors.[21]

> The Commonwealth [of Massachusetts] has disfavored the self-settled trust as a tool to protect one's assets from creditors, as it is seen as an attempt by a settlor to have his cake and eat it, too... it would violate established authority and public policy for an individual to have an estate to live on, but not an estate from which his debts could be paid.[22]

The Restatement of Trusts (a standard written by legal scholars to give state legislatures a model for adoption) and the Uniform Trust Code both reject the proposition that a self-settled spendthrift trust should allow a person a safe harbor from creditors.[23]

Notwithstanding the vehemence of those supporting the status quo, momentum seems to be in favor of the self-settled spendthrift trust.

Indeed, before the ink had even dried on Alaska's law, and in the same year Alaska passed its legislation, Delaware passed its own

---

[20] *Id.*

[21] *Phillips v. Moore*, 286 Ga. 619, 620, 690 S.E.2d 620, 621 (2010).

[22] *De Prins v. Michaeles*, 486 Mass. 41, 47, 154 N.E.3d 921, 927 (2020) (internal quotation marks and citations omitted).

[23] RESTATEMENT (THIRD) OF TRUSTS § 58(2) (2003) ("A restraint on the voluntary and involuntary alienation of a beneficial interest retained by the [grantor] of a trust is invalid."); UNIF. TRUST CODE § 505(a)(2) (follows the Restatement (Third) of Trusts and traditional doctrine that a grantor may not use the trust as a shield against the grantor's creditors).

version of the law.[24] Two years later, Nevada followed suit.[25] By 2018, fourteen other states (Hawaii, Michigan, Mississippi, Missouri, New Hampshire, Ohio, Oklahoma, Rhode Island, South Dakota, Tennessee, Utah, Virginia, West Virginia and Wyoming) had created some version of the self-settled asset protection trust, bringing the total to seventeen.[26]

In the last four years, Indiana,[27] Connecticut,[28] Alabama,[29] and Arkansas[30] have joined the growing list. In the 26 years since the first trust was introduced, 21 states have embraced some version of what has colloquially become known as the asset protection trust. If the trend continues, those who favor it will soon be in the majority.

Full Faith and Credit v. Conflict of Laws

We already discussed the Full Faith and Credit Clause of the U.S. Constitution[31] and how it guarantees that every state must recognize the laws of every other state, though not at the expense of enforcing its own laws.

If you live in a state with a statutory mechanism for creating a self-settled trust, it will likely honor such a trust coming from any other state (like if you live in Wyoming and have a Nevada asset protection trust).

But if you live in a state that does not have its own version and you set up an asset protection trust in one that does, there is less certainty as to how much protection the asset protection trust will provide.

For example, if you live in Washington (a state that does not have its own version of the asset protection trust), and you set up an Alaska asset protection trust, there is precedent that does not favor you.

That case, *In re Huber*, details how Washington resident Donald Huber was experiencing financial troubles, so he created an Alaska

---

[24] 80 Del. Laws, c. 153 § 5.
[25] NRS 166. Nevada emerged as a popular choice because of its relatively short statute of limitations. Generally, two years after a transfer into an asset protection trust, the transfer can no longer be challenged. *See* NRS 166.170.
[26] American Academy of Estate Planning Attorneys, "What is a DAPT?", available at https://www.aaepa.com/2019/01/domestic-asset-protection-trusts, last accessed August 22, 2023.
[27] I.C. 30-4-8.
[28] Conn. Gen. Stat. § 45a-487j.
[29] Ala. Code §8-9B-1 et seq.
[30] Ark. Code Ann. § 28-72-702(a).
[31] *See* discussion of the U.S. Constitution starting on page 132.

asset protection trust. He then transferred several million dollars of assets, including 13 development projects and several shopping centers, into the newly formed trust.[32] Following that transfer, he filed for bankruptcy.[33]

This case did not have good optics for the debtor. Although the court could likely have invalidated the transfer on grounds that it was fraudulent because the debtors were known at the time of the transfer, their analysis hinged on the relationship between the assets of the trust and the state of Alaska. Indeed, the court concluded that Alaska law, not Washington law, would have been upheld if Alaska had had "a substantial relation to the trust."[34]

Because the trustor, the beneficiaries, the creditors, all the assets of the trust but one certificate of deposit, and the attorney who drafted the trust were all in Washington, the court concluded that it was Washington law, not Alaskan law that ruled the day.[35]

The writing was on the wall for Donald Huber. Everything about his transaction was tied to Washington, and he didn't adopt this asset-protection strategy until creditors were knocking on his door. He had no hope.

But with some foresight, and a little planning, you could fare better. Although there are never any guarantees in the law, the trend is for more and more states to adopt provisions favoring the asset protection trust. And even if you live in a state that hasn't yet, your court knows what's trending in the law.

But you aren't just tossing the dice if you are taken to court over your trust. There are steps you can take to maximize your chances of a win.

For one, I do not recommend placing real estate that is located in a non-asset protection trust state into an asset protection trust. Instead, place it in an LLC. Regardless of where the LLC is formed, your state recognizes its validity and has its own version of the LLC.

Instead, I prefer the asset protection trust for liquid assets. Assets that aren't tied to your state (or any state—most liquid assets nowadays exist in the cloud). And if you have a broker in the same state as your asset protection trust, all the better. If the property at issue in an asset protection trust is not located in your state, a court in your state does not have as strong of a claim over it.

---

[32] *In re Huber*, 493 B.R. 798, 804–05 (Bankr. W.D. Wash. 2013).
[33] *Id.* at 806.
[34] *Id.* at 808.
[35] *Id.* at 809.

Additionally, hire an attorney from the state where the asset protection trust will be formed. Assign a trustee in that state. The more ties you have to the asset-protection trust state, the better your chances will be if someone tries to challenge the trust or the transfer.

As it stands, no matter where you live in the U.S., the asset protection trust is emerging as a viable and powerful tool in any asset-protection strategy.

PART III

Protecting Your Income

(Reducing Your Taxes)

CHAPTER 14

Paying the Minimum Self-Employment Taxes

Tax strategies are not about figuring out ways to avoid paying taxes. There are only two legal ways short of dying that I know of to avoid paying taxes altogether: (1) earning less than the standard deduction, which at present is $13,850 ($27,700 for married couples filing jointly), and (2) moving to a country that doesn't have income tax and earning all your income from sources in that country.[1] Those strategies probably don't appeal to too many U.S. doctors.

There are legitimate ways to set up a tax-free retirement if you pay all your taxes during your earning years. You aren't avoiding them there, but you are eliminating them during your retirement. But that's the subject of another book.[2]

Our focus here is not on eliminating taxes. It's on figuring out exactly what the tax code requires of you and paying that and no more. And structuring your medical practices and personal lives in such a way that the tax code's demands of you are the least amount possible.

---

[1] Even this won't guarantee you don't pay taxes. In most cases, you have to give up your U.S. citizenship as part of the strategy, which will in many cases trigger an expatriation tax. If Puerto Rico is your destination of choice, you can keep your citizenship and avoid the tax, but any income you continue to earn from the mainland will still be subject to taxation. Jon Zefi, et al., Eisner Amber, March 5, 2022, "Is Relocating to Puerto Rico the Right Move for You?" available at https://www.eisneramper.com/insights/tax/puerto-rico-tax-0321, last accessed August 23, 2023.

[2] One I already wrote: Parry, Z., *Unshackled: How to Escape the Chains of Conventional Wisdom that Keep You Poor*.Boss Media: New York (2020).

The first thing we'll look at is payroll taxes, which, for business owners, we call self-employment taxes.

As a doctor who has set up your healthcare business appropriately, there are two ways to pay yourself: (1) with a salary/wages, like any other employee, and (2) by distributing profits in the business.

Everything you pay yourself, whether via salary or distribution, is taxable as income,[3] so for income tax purposes, it doesn't matter how you choose to pay yourself. You'll be paying the same in income taxes either way.

However, everything you pay yourself as a salary is subject to the 15.3% self-employment taxes (FICA, Social Security, and Medicare),[4] just like it is with every other employee (the fact that the employee pays half doesn't help you here where you are both the employer and the employee, so you're paying both halves when you pay yourself).

The valuable lesson here is that you aren't paying any of those payroll taxes when you distribute profits from the business to you.

The income taxes on $200,000 in income (regardless of whether it comes as salary or distribution), assuming you are a single filer and have no deductions beyond the standard non-itemized deduction, is about $38,400 in federal taxes plus some in-state taxes if you live in a state that collects those.

If you take all $200,000 as a salary, then another $30,600 (15.3%) will be taken out of your check before you even get paid.

If you take all $200,000 as a distribution, then that $30,600 in payroll taxes gets reduced to zero because you don't pay self-employment taxes on distributions.[5]

Seems like a no-brainer then, right? If you pay yourself a salary, your net after taxes is $131,000, but if it's a distribution, you get to keep $161,600. Why would any doctor who owns a business ever pay themselves a salary when they can pay distributions?

Because the IRS says if you work for your medical practice, you have to pay yourself a salary.[6]

---

[3] 26 U.S.C. § 61.
[4] 26 U.S.C. § 1401. There is an additional 0.9% in taxes for those who make over a certain threshold. In 2023, it is $250,000 for joint returns. *Id.* §1401(2)(A).
[5] *H B & R, Inc. v. United States*, 229 F.3d 688, 690 (8th Cir. 2000) ("The employer's obligation to withhold extends only to an employee's wages. It does not apply to other types of employee income, such as dividends...")
[6] *See, e.g., Texas Carbonate Co. v. Phinney*, 307 F.2d 289, 291 (5th Cir. 1962) (applying employer-employee tests to determine if officer of corporation is an employee).

They know this potential loophole much better than you do. But the government insists on getting its payroll taxes, so they've created a rule that prevents you from paying yourself purely in distributions.

Unfortunately, the rule is not written out neatly in the tax code, but rather is a hodgepodge of pieces from different sections of the code and different IRS Rulings, Treasury Regulations, and cases.[7]

If we distill its separate parts into a simple rule, it says, in effect, that regardless of how you classify the payment to yourself, the employee-business owner (whether that payment be a salary, distribution, bonus, or other remuneration), self-employment taxes must be paid on the reasonable value of the services rendered. In simpler terms, whatever your services are worth, that's what you'll owe taxes on, irrespective of what wages you choose to pay yourself.

Let's simplify that even more: figure out what a reasonable salary would be for someone doing your job, pay yourself that salary (assuming the business makes enough to pay it), and then pay everything else in distributions.

In theory it sounds simple, but figuring out what a reasonable salary is could get a bit complicated. Suppose you ever do get audited, and the IRS challenges the salary you've chosen to pay yourself. In that instance, these are the factors and questions that will be considered to determine whether you've paid yourself correctly, or whether you owe the IRS (or less likely, whether they owe you):

- Employee's role in the company
  - Position held by employee
  - Hours worked
  - Duties performed

- Comparison to similarly situated employees in other companies
  - If employee is performing work of three people, then would need to compare to combined salaries of three positions in another company

---

[7] *See* 26 U.S.C. 162(a)(1) (defining reasonable compensation for purposes of an allowance of deductible business expenses); Rev. Rul. 74-44, 1974-1 C.B. 287 (1974) (applying the concept of reasonable cases to self-employment tax cases);
26 C.F.R. § 1.162-7 (distinguishing between salaries paid for services rendered and other compensation); *David E. Watson, P.C. v. United States*, 668 F.3d 1008, 1017 (8th Cir. 2012) (applying reasonable compensation rule to self-employment tax cases).

- Character and condition of company
    o Company's size as indicated by sales, net income, or capital value
    o Complexities of the business
    o General economic conditions

- Conflicts of interest
    o Does a relationship exist between the employer and the employee that might permit the employee to disguise wages as other forms of compensation? (In self-employment situations, the answer is always going to be "yes.")

- Internal consistency
    o Is employee paid proportionately with other employees in the same company?
    o Are bonuses awarded under a structured, formal, consistently applied program?
    o Is compensation an indication of ownership rather than services provided?[8]

Basically, if you were not the owner of the company and were to get paid a reasonable salary for the services you provide to the company, what would that salary be? Whatever that salary is determined to be is the amount the self-employment taxes will be based on.

So the best practice is to create a fair salary for yourself, pay it, and then take the rest in distributions. That ensures both that you are complying with the law but not paying any more in taxes than is your due.

Let's suppose that you are a dentist. You perform the ordinary duties of a dentist. Because you're a small business owner, not a large corporation, you are also the human resource manager and handle the marketing for your practice.

To determine an appropriate salary, you would have to take all of that into account.

You understand dentists in your area with your experience and credentials typically make about $250,000 per year. The other

---

[8] *Elliotts, Inc. v. Comm'r*, 716 F.2d 1241, 1245–48 (9th Cir. 1983).

dentists in your office, who are not as experienced as you are, are earning about $200,000 per year.

You know a human resource manager who handles HR for a chain of dental offices who earns about $65,000 annually.

You have sought bids from marketing agencies and know it will take about $5,000 per month to outsource your marketing.

Need help determining your reasonable salary? Check out the salary statistics on the Bureau of Labor and Statistics' website[9] or do some searching on employer-reviewed sites like Glass Door.[10]

That's your starting point. Now we work from there.

How are you different from the other dentists making $250,000? Are you working fewer hours than they are? Reduce it accordingly. Do you specialize in something they do not? You might be more valuable then. Do your other dentists get raises at the end of every year? Then you're going to give yourself one, too.

What about compensation for your HR duties? The HR manager you know works full time, but you probably only spend four hours per month on HR responsibilities because you don't hire very often and only have a few employees. Plus, HR isn't your specialty, so you aren't worth as much as someone trained in HR. So you're going to pay yourself far less than the $65,000 the full-time HR manager gets.

You'll go through a similar exercise for marketing. You only spend a few hours a month, and you don't really know what you're doing. You can justify paying yourself a lot less than the pros at the agency.

Go through this exercise and document it so if the IRS ever comes knocking, you'll be able to show them how you arrived at your salary. If you can show that your reasoning makes sense, it probably won't go any farther.

Let's say then, that after you go through this analysis, you decide that you should pay yourself $235,000 as a dentist (you are more specialized than others, but you work one fewer day a week than they do), $2,500 annually for your HR duties, and $6,500 annually for the marketing. You've calculated a reasonable annual salary for yourself of $244,000.

Payday is twice per month, so every paycheck you get $10,166.66. Any profits your business generates after that can be paid as distributions, which means as your business gets more profitable, you take home a bigger chunk of your income without paying the 15.3%

---

[9] https://www.bls.gov/bls/blswage.htm.
[10] https://glassdoor.com.

in self-employment taxes. You know exactly how much you need to pay, and you've empowered yourself not to pay a penny more.

What if Your Business Does Not Make Enough to Pay Your Reasonable Salary?

If you've arrived at $244,000 as a reasonable salary for your services, but after paying all your other expenses, there is not enough left in the business to pay that salary, what then?

The IRS is not going to make you pay using money you don't have. So if you can only afford to pay yourself $50,000 the first year because the business just started, that's what you're going to pay yourself. It's all going to be salary. You aren't going to pay yourself any distributions at all until you've hit that salary benchmark. After that, it's all distributions. And that's where you want to be because distributions are more tax-advantaged than your salary.

What if Your Business Is Really Successful and You Have Enough to Pay Far More Distributions Than Salary?

Let's consider the other extreme. Your reasonable salary is $244,000, but the business brings in enough money that you could pay yourself $2,000,000?

The same rules apply. You pay yourself your $244,000 salary, and then the rest is a distribution, which is a share of the profits. You'll pay the 15.3% in self-employment taxes on the $244,000 only. And, of course, you'll still report all of it as income.

How Does This Knowledge Save You in Taxes?

The idea here is the same with any other kind of taxes—find that point where you are paying exactly what you owe and no more. If your reasonable salary is $244,000, but you're only paying yourself a salary of $150,000, and therefore saving 15.3% on the difference ($94,000), then it may feel like you're saving money, but if you ever get audited, you'll end up paying all the back taxes, plus penalties and interest. And depending on the circumstances, you might be facing criminal charges, too.

But you also don't want to pay too much. If you're giving yourself a $500,000 salary, but you only have to be paying $244,000, you are giving up over $39,000 in taxes that you don't have to.

Figure out what your salary should be. Then pay it. You'll save 15.3% on everything else (the distributions). And you'll be safe if you're ever audited.

When You Might Want to Pay More in Salary than You Have To

So far, in the salary v. distribution analysis, we've just been looking at it from a tax perspective. And if the only thing you had to worry about is taxes, that's all the advice you'd need: figure out what your salary should be, then only pay self-employment taxes on that amount.

But taxes are just one consideration. If you are thinking of buying a house in the next couple of years, for example, your priorities might change.

When qualifying for a home loan as a business owner, different rules apply to you than if you were a W2 employee working for someone else. It's a lot more complicated, and among other differences, your salary counts for a lot more than dividends do, so in some situations, it might make sense to bump up the salary and reduce the dividends. The IRS is never going to complain if you pay more than you need to in self-employment taxes. Consult with a mortgage lender who specializes in loans to business owners to figure out whether this would be advantageous to you based on the price range you're looking for and your current salary.

CHAPTER 15

Tax Strategies for Business Owners

It should come as no surprise to you that owning a business affords you far more options when it comes to tax strategies than if all of your income is reported on a W2. You may not have your own medical practice at the moment. The good news is you don't have to have a health center, employ healthcare and office workers, or register patients to become a business owner.

Are you paid as a 1099? You're a business owner.

Are you paid as a W2 but you invest in real estate on the side? You're a business owner. Invest in anything on the side? Business owner.

You may not have structured yourself like a business owner, but if you are paid as an independent contractor or do any sort of investing or consulting, you can set yourself up to get many of the same tax advantages as any other small business owner. For example, if you contract to a telemedicine firm, a hospital, or a pharmaceutical company, you could still reap tax benefits.[1]

The purpose of this chapter is not to provide an exhaustive list of tax strategies available to small business owners, but to help you understand how tax strategies work. In the process, we will also identify some of the low-hanging fruit—those strategies that apply to most business owners, are easy to implement, and will make a noticeable difference in the amount of taxes you pay.

---

[1] If you want more information on how to do that, drop me a line: zach@thefortunelawfirm.com.

But first, let's make sure we're speaking the same language.

How Taxes Work

Although one look at any section of the tax code will have you feeling dizzy at its complexity,[2] in function, taxation is relatively simple.

We start with your gross income, reduce it by your deductions, and then you pay taxes based on the tax bracket published for the current tax year.

Because ours is a progressive or graduated tax system, your tax bracket defines the highest tax rate you pay on all the income above the threshold of the tax bracket. You don't pay that rate on all your income. For example, if you are in the 22% tax bracket for 2023, that means you make at least $44,725 but no more than $95,375 (for a single person, after deductions).[3]

If you make $64,725 in taxable income, then you only pay 22% on the last $20,000 of your income (the $20,000 in that bracket). The first $44,725 gets taxed at lower rates corresponding with the ranges defined by the tax brackets.

For 2023 rates, $33,725 of that gets taxed at 12%, and $11,000 gets taxed at 10%. Here's the total tax rate for someone with taxable income of $64,725 (i.e., after deductions):

Amount	Tax Rate	Taxes
$11,000	10%	$1,100.00
$33,725	12%	$3,777.20
$20,000	22%	$4,400.00
$64,725	15.28%	$9,277.20

If your taxable income is $64,725, and you're a single filer, your taxes due will be $9,277.20, which is 15.28% of your taxable income (which is a weighted average of all your income amounts at each

---

[2] Go ahead. Look at any section of Title 26 of the United States Code. Or start at the very beginning, 26 U.S.C. § 1. The tables at the top seem pretty straightforward. But then scroll down to where it starts explaining the "phaseout of marriage penalty." It's enough to cure insomnia.
[3] Durante, A. "2023 Tax Brackets," *Tax Foundation*, October 17, 2022, available at https://taxfoundation.org/data/all/federal/2023-tax-brackets, last accessed August 23, 2023.

bracketed tax rate). With this calculation, tax deductions are already taken into account, though if there are tax credits, you could be entitled to additional offsets. Let's walk through how that works.

Let's continue with this example. With the numbers we have, we don't know what the actual income or deductions were. All single filers in 2023 are entitled to at least the $13,850 standard deduction, so we know this filer had at least $78,575 in income (the $64,725 in taxable income plus the $13,850 standard deduction).

If that were the only deduction claimed, then the effective tax rate would have been 11.8%.[4]

Let's suppose, though, that this filer made use of several tax reductions other than the standard deduction. They took advantage of the Augusta tax savings method (more on that in a minute), their home office deduction, and a § 179 deduction for the purchase of office equipment.[5] Perhaps they took home $94,000, but $10,000 of that was not counted as income because it was a reimbursement under the Augusta method, and between the home office and equipment purchases, they qualify for another $5,425 in deductions. That gets them to $78,575, which is further reduced by the standard deduction, so even though they're taking home $94,000, they're only getting taxed on $64,725 of it, which means their taxes are still $9,277.20.

Now their effective tax rate is an enviable 9.87%. They might as well be in the lowest bracket for all their income!

Now suppose they have two children that qualify them for $2,000 in tax credits for each child.[6] That's $4,000 we just shave right off the final tax bill, so now they only owe $5,277.20, which is an effective tax rate of 5.61%!

This example helps illustrate the difference between a tax deduction and a tax credit. A tax deduction reduces your taxable income and saves you as much in taxes as the deduction multiplied by your highest tax bracket.

In the simplest version of our scenario, where the only deduction claimed was the standard deduction, taxable income was reduced by

---

[4] That's $9,277.20 divided by $78,575.
[5] Each of these is discussed in greater detail below.
[6] *See* IRS.gov, "Child Tax Credit," available at https://www.irs.gov/credits-deductions/individuals/child-tax-credit, last accessed August 23, 2023.

$13,850, and because the highest tax bracket was 22%, that resulted in tax savings of $3,047.[7]

A tax credit, on the other hand, reduces your taxes dollar for dollar. If $13,850 in deductions saves you $3,047, and $4,000 in credits saves you $4,000, you can see that a tax credit gives you more bang for your buck than a tax deduction.

With any tax-reduction plan, then, we're going to look for at least three types of savings (1) ways to recharacterize money you receive so it isn't considered taxable, (2) deductions that apply to reduce your taxable income, and (3) tax credits that will directly reduce your calculated tax bill.

Although there are potentially several from each category available to you, we will highlight just a few.

The Augusta Rule

Whether you own a dental practice, family practice, or other healthcare-related business (or indeed, any sort of business), if you work for your business, you must pay yourself a salary, and beyond that, you can pay yourself distributions from the business.[8] Although one requires self-employment taxes and the other does not, they both count as income, so whether it's salary or distribution, it all is taxable.[9]

But did you know that there are ways for you to transfer money from your business account to your personal account that do not count as taxable income at all?

The Augusta Rule, in its simplest form, allows you to rent out your home, and fourteen days of rental income is not taxable.[10] This rule was originally designed to give tax benefits to the residents of Augusta, Georgia who would rent out their homes for two weeks per year to host visitors to the Masters Tournament.[11]

---

[7] If the tax deduction serves to lower the taxpayer into a lower bracket, then the savings is a little harder to calculate as you have to account for two parts of the deduction at two different taxable rates.

[8] And if you didn't know before reading this book, you know now after reading Chapter 14.

[9] 26 U.S.C. § 61.

[10] 26 U.S.C. § 280A.

[11] Vlad Rusz, Forbes, February 27, 2023, "How Business Owners Can Use the Augusta Rule Tax Strategy," available at
https://www.forbes.com/sites/forbesfinancecouncil/2023/02/28/how-business-owners-can-use-the-augusta-rule-tax-strategy/, last accessed August 23, 2023.

You can take advantage of the same rule and take advantage of tax-free rental income the same way, though if you're a business owner, there is a much better way to do it.

Keep in mind, though, that if your home is your primary place of business, you can't use this tax strategy.[12]

The rule does not require renting your home out to strangers or for an overnight stay. Instead, you can rent your home out for any legitimate business purpose.

If you're a business owner, those purposes come easy. You've got staff, and you hold regular trainings.[13] Instead of cramming them all in the break room or renting out a place from someone else, why not have your business rent out your house so you can hold those trainings at your home? Getting employees out of the office is good for morale. Plus, you've got a barbecue at your house, plenty of seating, a large-screen television, and Wi-Fi—everything you need to host a great meeting.

The rule allows you to host the meetings at your house and invoice your business for use of the house. Your business then pays you, and that money is not taxable.

But how much do you charge?

There is no chart or diagram telling us what the allowable cost per square foot is in any given city. But it's got to be reasonable. So do your market research.

Let's say you need a space that will accommodate eight people, have audiovisual equipment, have Wi-Fi, and permit you to bring your own food. Call a couple of hotels to see what it would cost to rent out a conference room. Look up homes on Airbnb or VRBO to see what they're going for in your area.

If you're only going to use the main floor and back yard of your home, look for a place similarly sized. How much would it cost you to get something like that in the marketplace?

That's how much you can charge. Maybe give your business a little discount.

It's best to have a rental agreement in place between you and your business, actually send invoices to your business, and then have your business pay the invoices. Keep minutes of the meetings. Take pictures. Make sure it's all well documented so if you get audited you can justify the tax strategy.

---

[12] *Id.*

[13] Remember from Chapter 11—those trainings that prevent you being liable for your employees' mistakes.

At the end of the year, your business is going to issue a 1099 to you, and then your tax preparer will report it on your tax return as non-taxable income, excused under IRC § 280A.

How much in taxes can this save you? If you collect $1,200 to rent out your house, and you do that fourteen times per year, that's $16,800 you can collect in rental income that isn't taxable. If you're in the 32% tax bracket, you've saved yourself $5,376 in taxes. You've also saved a bit in gas by holding the meetings at your home. Not bad.

The Home Office Deduction

The home office deduction is simple: if you own a business and use a portion of your home *exclusively* and *regularly* for work purposes, you may be able to deduct a portion of your home-office-related expenses.[14] So if you always work from your medical practice, you need to change your working habits or skip this section!

First, let's make sure you qualify.

Exclusive: There must be some area of your home, identifiable as separate (though permanent partitions are not required) that you use exclusively for your business[15]. If during work hours it's your office and at night and on weekends your kids use it for homework, it's not exclusive use.

Regular: It must also be used regularly. Even if a room or space is designated exclusively for work, it's not enough to qualify if you never or rarely use it. There is no hard-line standard for what constitutes "regular use," except that its use cannot merely be "occasional" or "incidental."[16]

Trade or Business Use: Its exclusive and business use has to be connected to a trade or business.[17] Managing your own day trades is not enough. It must be connected to a legitimate business.

If you've made it this far, you are most of the way there. Now that you have a portion of your home for exclusive and regular business use, you've got to meet at least one of three additional requirements:

---

[14] For the official IRS ins and outs of the home office deduction, take a look at IRS Publication 587, "Business Use of Your Home," available at https://www.irs.gov/pub/irs-pdf/p587.pdf, last accessed August 23, 2023.
[15] *Id.* at 3. There are exceptions to the exclusive use rule: (1) if its use is for the storage of inventory or product samples, or (2) if it's used as a daycare. *Id.*
[16] *Id.*
[17] *Id.*

either (1) it is your primary place of business, (2) you meet patients, clients, or customers in your home, or (3) it is a separate structure.[18]

Do you qualify? If so, what are the benefits?

Like many tax deductions, you've got options here. You can either calculate actual expenses or use a simpler standard amount.

For the standard amount, you get $5 for every square foot of your home office, up to $1,500 (i.e., up to 300 square feet).[19]

To calculate the expenses, first you need to figure out if the expense is directly related to your home office, indirectly related, or not related at all.

Directly related: costs and expenses for just the home office.[20] If you repaint the home office or fix a crack in its window, those costs are directly related to the home office, and you can deduct 100% of those.

Indirectly related: costs and expenses for the entire home. This includes insurance, utilities, security systems, real estate taxes, mortgage interest, depreciation, and general repairs.[21] You can deduct a portion of these expenses.

Unrelated: costs associated with parts of your home unrelated to your business, like lawn care.[22] You cannot claim any part of these expenses.

The next part of the equation is figuring out what portion of your home is used exclusively and regularly for business use. If your home is 3,000 square feet, and your home office is 300 square feet, then you can deduct 10% of the indirect costs.[23]

Suppose you do the math and realize that you've expended $800 in direct costs, $28,000 in indirect costs, and $1,200 in unrelated costs.

Your home office deduction is going to be $800 (you get all the direct costs), plus $2,800 (10% of the indirect costs).[24] You don't get to deduct the unrelated costs. So your total deduction is $3,600. As long as your gross income from the business use of your home exceeds your total business expenses, you get to deduct the full amount.[25]

Remember, your deduction amount is not the amount you save in taxes. If you're in the 32% tax bracket, the $3,600 deduction shaves $1,152 off your tax bill.

---

[18] *Id.* at 3–4.
[19] *Id.* at 10.
[20] *Id.* at 6.
[21] *Id.*
[22] *Id.*
[23] *Id.* at 9.
[24] *Id.* at 6.
[25] *Id.* at 9.

That's not the biggest tax strategy available, but if it takes you 30 minutes to gather the information to make your calculations, the U.S. government just paid you over $2,000/hour for your trouble!

Hire Your Children

If you've got kids (or grandkids), hiring them as employees could save you in taxes while teaching them a good work ethic. It's a win-win.[26]

The premise behind this strategy is that since you are in a higher tax bracket than your kids, if you can transfer some of your income to them, the overall tax burden will be lower.

This only makes sense if you're going to be spending money on your kids anyway (and let's be honest, that's where all your money goes).

Consider this scenario: Your business pays you $200,000, and you've got another $200,000 left in the business at the end of the year in profits that you have to pay taxes on.[27]

You've got $400,000 in taxable income to start, which you whittle down to $340,000 using various deductions.

Now let's suppose you have three minor children you hire to work for you. The two oldest clean your office twice per week, take attendance and photographs at the monthly meetings you hold at your house, and come in several times a week to scan and shred documents.

Your youngest isn't quite old enough to have responsibilities like that, but she does join her older siblings for the photo shoots where you use the kids as models to promote your business.

You pay your older kids $10,000 per year each, and your youngest $5,000.[28] Whatever you pay them, it's got to be reasonable for the value they're providing.

Now, you pay yourself $200,000, and, having paid the kids, you've only got $175,000 left in the account at the end of the year that drops to your personal taxes. That's $375,000 in income, which you whittle

---

[26] What do you mean, you couldn't work with your kids? ;)
[27] Huston, H, "S corp (s corporation) advantages & disadvantages," July 20, 2022, available at https://www.wolterskluwer.com/en/expert-insights/s-corporation-advantages-and-disadvantages (last visited August 23, 2023).
[28] I am making these numbers up. I have no idea what models charge, having never been solicited by others to have my likeness on display for the purpose of making money. Their loss. Before deciding how much to pay your kids, you'll want to look into stuff like that.

down to $315,000 after those same deductions. You're in the 32% tax bracket, so you've saved yourself $8,000 in taxes.

Your kids, who have made $10,000, $10,000, and $5,000, respectively (you're their only source of income), won't owe any income taxes because they've all made less than the standard deduction of $13,850.

Hopefully you're teaching your kids money management at this point. We use Greenlight[29] at our house, which is a debit card made for kids that helps them learn responsible spending (and gives you full control and notifications for all purchases).

Now your kids are purchasing their own school clothes and contributing to the price of the new trampoline in the backyard. You've just taken some of the money you spent on them that was after-tax money and turned it into a tax deduction. And your kids are learning important life lessons, too.

The next year, you up your game. Instead of giving them their entire paycheck in cash, you set up a cash-value life insurance contract for them. Or a Roth IRA.[30] Your kids have benefits!

The payment is still tax-deductible to your business, and what would have been taxable income for them is not because they're still making below the standard deduction. The money that goes into these accounts accumulates tax-free, so they'll have liquidity and tax advantages in one. You've just set up an account where they didn't pay taxes on the money going in, won't pay taxes on the growth, and will never pay taxes on the money coming out. Wow!

How Else Can You Save?

Although in principle, calculating taxes is a relatively simple process—start with your income, apply deductions and credits, and then run your taxable income through the tax code—in practice, *taxes are complicated.*

---

[29] Greenlight.com.
[30] You will want them contributing money themselves to the IRA from their earnings. If it is an employer-sponsored plan, things could get complicated because you have to make sure you are treating all employees equally. IRS.gov "401(k) Plan Fix-It Guide—The Plan Failed the 401(k) ADP and ACP Nondiscrimination Tests," available at https://www.irs.gov/retirement-plans/401k-plan-fix-it-guide-the-plan-failed-the-401k-adp-and-acp-nondiscrimination-tests, last accessed August 24, 2023.

By one estimate, the tax code, including both the United States Code and IRS regulations, was roughly 4 million words as of 2012.[31] And considering that, on average, there is one change per day to the tax code,[32] you can imagine how complicated it can be to apply it.

Just as with the language used in the NPDB regulations, the words used by Congress and the IRS to set the tax rules are the same words we must adhere to when filing, reporting, and paying our taxes. Similarly, the IRS must follow those words when seeking to enforce the tax code. And given the sheer girth of tax law (the entire Harry Potter series comes in at about 25% of the length of the tax code),[33] there are an abundance of opportunities to use the tax code to our advantage.

Some, like the ones I have outlined, may be low-hanging fruit. Some may readily apply to your situation without much more than keeping documentation. Some require some work on your part to apply, perhaps the creation of an entity, conducting an engineering study, hiring scientific specialists to analyze the innovation in your practice, purchasing equipment, or setting up an employee health program at work.

Some only apply to business owners, some to homeowners, some to daycare owners. There are tax savings for real estate investors, crypto investors, and farmers. As you are all too aware, our legislators have yet to carve out tax savings specific to doctors.[34] But there are a whole host of them meant for business owners in any field.

Some tax deductions save you a little in the short term but cost you more along the way and require careful strategizing to ensure they don't cost you extra in the long run.[35]

To take advantage of the full gamut of tax strategies that might be available to you, you really need to sit down with someone (not a

---

[31] Bishop-Henchman, J. "How Many Words Are in the Tax Code?", Tax Foundation, April 15, 2014, available at https://taxfoundation.org/blog/how-many-words-are-tax-code, last accessed August 24, 2023.
[32] *Id.*
[33] The entire Harry Potter series is not just shorter at approximately 1,000,000 words, it is also far more likely to be read. Perhaps we should have had JK Rowling draft the tax code for us. *See id.*
[34] Don't hold your breath for that. It's not going to happen anytime soon.
[35] Contributions to a qualified plan like a 401k or deferring tax payment through a 1031 exchange are two examples. Whenever you hear of a tax strategy that consists of deferring tax payments now in exchange for paying them later, be cautious of a trap.

CPA!)[36] who both understands taxes and doctors. It will be worth it almost no matter what the cost because chances are you are overpaying in taxes.

And hey, if you think the government is doing an exceptional job, then by all means, tip them. They won't thank you, but they'll certainly take it.

---

[36] CPAs are tax preparers. They are not tax reducers. For a more in-depth discussion, see Chapter 11 of my book *Unshackled: How to Escape the Chains of Conventional Wisdom that Keep You Poor*, Boss Media: New York (2020).

PART IV

Protecting Your Legacy

CHAPTER 16

The Revocable Living Trust

As a medical professional, you are likely more familiar with mortality than most. Even if you aren't seeing life-threatening injuries or terminal patients, your expertise is the human body, and you know how frail life is.

Accidents, illnesses, injury, and death are a part of life that often get in the way of life. And although we can't eliminate injury and death completely (not yet, anyway!), there are steps we can take to make sure when they happen, we are as legally prepared as we can be. The best legal tool for that is the revocable living trust.

A revocable trust has two major purposes: to work for you while you are alive and to work for you after death. These two purposes, performed by the same "living" document, look very different, depending on whether your heart is still beating.

Before we examine these purposes in detail, let's take a step back and identify what a revocable trust is, what it isn't, and who the involved parties are.

First, we need to be clear on the fact that there are an infinite number of ways a trust can be created, and they can have any of a number of purposes, trustees, and functions. Black's Law Dictionary defines 261 terms that include the word "trust."[1]

---

[1] Its first entry is "2503(b) Trust," which is "a trust that requires a distribution of income to the beneficiary at least annually, and provides that gifts to the trust qualifying as gifts of a present interest become eligible for the annual gift-tax exclusion." The last, a "wasting trust," is "a trust in which the trust property is

A trust, in a general sense, is "the right, enforceable solely in equity, to the beneficial enjoyment of property to which another person holds the legal title; a property interest held by one person (the trustee) at the request of another (the settlor) for the benefit of a third party (the beneficiary)."[2]

That, like most legal definitions, probably doesn't do much for you, so let's throw in some legal explication:

> Some courts and legal writers have defined a trust as a certain kind of right that the beneficiary has against the trustee, or a certain kind of interest that the beneficiary has against the trustee, or a certain kind of interest that the beneficiary has in the trust property, thus looking at it from the point of view of the beneficiary. While it is true that the beneficiary has the right or interest described, the trust is something more than the right or interest of the beneficiary. The trust is the whole juridical device: the legal relationship between the parties with respect to the property that is its subject matter, including not merely the duties that the trustee owes to the beneficiary and to the rest of the world, but also the rights, privileges, powers, and immunities that the beneficiary has against the trustee and against the rest of the world. It would seem proper, therefore, to define the trust either as a relationship having certain characteristics stated in the definition or perhaps as a juridical device or legal institution involving such a relationship.[3]

That might have shed some light on it for you, or perhaps you're starting to realize why you picked up a book to learn this stuff instead of researching the law on your own.

Let's use an example of a common scenario where the existence of a trust solves a problem that would be very difficult, if even possible, to solve without one. We'll use an example from my life.

---

gradually depleted by periodic payments to the beneficiary." TRUST, Black's Law Dictionary (11th ed. 2019).

[2] *Id.*

[3] Scott, AW & Fratcher, WF. *The Law of Trusts* § 2.4, at 42 (4th ed. 1987).

Example: The Special Needs Trust

My sister-in-law is an adult with special needs, subsisting on limited income because her mental capabilities restrict her job opportunities. To maintain her independence, she relies on three main pillars: her own modest earnings, financial assistance from family, and governmental support in the form of Supplemental Security Income (SSI). This arrangement is stable for as long as her family support network remains in place but raises concerns about what would happen should she outlive those who currently assist her.

Let's dissect her revenue streams:

1. **Employment Income**: Her job provides a consistent but limited income. As long as she's able to work, this will remain a source of funds.

2. **Family Support**: Our family contributes to cover unexpected expenses, like home and car maintenance. Additionally, her mother has a life insurance policy intended to provide continued financial backing after her passing.

3. **SSI Benefits**: She qualifies for SSI based on her disability status, medical history, and other criteria.[4] However, to maintain these benefits, she must pass a monthly resource test,[5] which calculates her total assets to ensure they don't exceed a certain limit.[6]

The last point is crucial, especially when considering what happens when her mother passes away. Upon her mother's death, the life insurance payout could disqualify her from SSI by making her assets exceed the allowable limit.[7] The funds would then have to be

---

[4] Social Security, "Understanding Supplemental Security Income if You Have a Disability or Are Blind—2023 Edition," available at https://www.ssa.gov/ssi/text-disable-ussi.htm, last accessed August 29, 2023.

[5] Social Security, "Understanding Supplemental Security Income SSI Resources—2023 Edition," available at https://www.ssa.gov/ssi/text-resources-ussi.htm, last accessed August 29, 2023.

[6] *Id.*

[7] *Id.* According to the Social Security Administration, "if the value of your resources that we count is over the allowable limit at the beginning of the month, you cannot receive SSI for that month."

expended before she could re-qualify for SSI, creating an incentive for rapid spending of the insurance payout.

To mitigate this issue, we have established a special needs trust. The life insurance proceeds will be channeled into this trust instead of going directly to her. Remember, a trust is a legal entity that holds and manages assets for the benefit of a third party. In this case, my mother-in-law (the settlor) has directed that upon her death, the insurance payout will go into a trust managed by my wife (the trustee) for the benefit of my sister-in-law (the beneficiary).

What does this look like in practice? A designated bank account will be created under the trust's name, and my wife, as the trustee, will oversee the funds according to the terms set by my mother-in-law.

This achieves two primary objectives:

1. **SSI Qualification**: Assets in a special needs trust do not count towards the SSI resource test,[8] allowing my sister-in-law to continue receiving these benefits.

2. **Structured Spending**: The trust's terms will specify allowable expenditures, such as home repairs or medical bills, ensuring the funds are used responsibly.

By doing this, we safeguard my sister-in-law's financial future without jeopardizing her SSI benefits.

This serves as a practical example of how trusts can be utilized for specific financial planning needs. We'll spend the remainder of this book discussing what is probably the most common kind of trust: a revocable living trust.

The Revocable Living Trust

A revocable living trust is a dynamic estate-planning instrument designed to offer maximum flexibility both during your lifetime and after your passing. Unlike a will, which only becomes effective upon your death, a revocable living trust starts working the moment it is created and assets are transferred into it. As the name suggests, it's "revocable," meaning you can alter or completely dissolve it as your

---

[8] Social Security, "Spotlight on Trusts—2023 Edition," available at https://www.ssa.gov/ssi/spotlights/spot-trusts.htm, last accessed August 29, 2023.

circumstances or intentions change. This ability to adapt is one of its most compelling features.

Remember from our definition above that a trust has a settlor, the trustee, and the beneficiary.

A revocable living trust is a legal entity created to hold and manage assets during the lifetime of the person who establishes it—the "settlor"—and to facilitate the transfer of these assets upon the settlor's death. One of the most compelling features of a revocable living trust is its flexibility; the settlor can amend or dissolve the trust as circumstances change.

During the settlor's lifetime, the trust can be beneficial in multiple ways. If the settlor becomes incapacitated, the trust provides a prearranged mechanism for financial and medical decisions, often eliminating the need for court-appointed guardianship. For these tasks, the "trustee" takes over. While the settlor is alive and well, they can serve as their own trustee, managing assets as they see fit. However, a successor trustee—often a trusted family member or financial institution—can be designated to take over the management responsibilities should the settlor become unable to do so.

Upon the settlor's death, the trust evolves from revocable to irrevocable, meaning it can no longer be changed. This is where the "beneficiary" comes into play. The beneficiary is the person, or group of persons, destined to receive the trust's assets. The trustee's role now shifts to ensuring that the trust's assets are distributed to the beneficiaries as outlined in the trust document, thereby bypassing the often cumbersome and costly probate process. This quick and private distribution is one of the key benefits of a revocable living trust.

At its core, a revocable living trust aims to achieve two primary objectives:

1. **Lifetime Management**: It serves as your financial advocate when you're incapacitated, streamlining important decisions related to guardianship, medical care, and financial management. This can encompass everything from power-of-attorney arrangements to specific medical directives.

2. **Estate Transition**: After your death, the trust ensures a smooth, court-free transition of your assets to the designated beneficiaries. This effectively sidesteps the often cumbersome and expensive probate process.

We'll devote the next two chapters to discussing these two objectives of a revocable living trust.

CHAPTER 17

The Revocable Living Trust – Speaking for You When You Cannot

A revocable living trust's first primary objective operates during your lifetime: to speak for you when you cannot speak for yourself. As a person with medical training, you will be only too aware of that possibility.

While you have all your mental and physical faculties,[1] let's ask you all of life's important questions. We can write down all the answers in a legal instrument that will have the authority to effectuate your wishes (through designees you select) should you be incapacitated or otherwise unable to act on your own behalf:

- Who do you want making financial decisions on your behalf?
- Who do you want making medical decisions on your behalf?
- Are there any medical procedures or treatments you never want (or always want) to receive in a given circumstance?
- Do you want your life prolonged by artificial means?
- Do you want to donate your organs?
- Who do you want taking care of you if you can no longer take care of yourself?
- Who do you want taking care of your minor children if you are no longer able to take care of them?

---

[1] Or at least most of them, depending on whether you're a party animal or a wellness guru.

- Do you have any preferences regarding your funeral service?
- How do you want your remains disposed of?

Let's dive into how a trust addresses each of these concerns.

General Power of Attorney

A general power of attorney is a legal document that empowers one person, known as the agent or attorney-in-fact, to act on behalf of another, called the principal, in various matters that can include financial transactions, property management, and legal decisions.[2]

Although the phrase "attorney-in-fact" might suggest that the appointed agent must be a lawyer, that's not the case; the agent can be a trusted friend, family member, or business associate. The principal must be of sound mind and legal age when executing the document to ensure its validity. In many jurisdictions, notarization and the presence of witnesses are often required for additional legality and enforceability.[3]

The scope of the authority granted under a general power of attorney is broad and can be both convenient and strategically important. For example, if someone anticipates being overseas and unable to manage their finances or make critical decisions about their property, a general power of attorney can give the appointed agent the necessary authority to handle these matters. Perhaps you want to head overseas and volunteer for a remote healthcare project where there won't be good connectivity? You might need a backup plan for decisions about your medical practice or rental properties at home. Additionally, the general power of attorney is often integral to estate planning, where it can serve as a contingency plan if the principal becomes incapacitated.

The power granted in a general power of attorney is often quite sweeping. The agent can generally manage all financial affairs, execute contracts, deal with real estate transactions, and even represent the principal in court.[4] It's crucial to note, however, that the agent is expected to act in the best interest of the principal, being governed by what's called a fiduciary duty. This duty obliges the agent to act with

---

[2] *E.g.*, 14 V.S.A. § 4002(5) and (9); § 4031(a).
[3] *E.g.*, 14 V.S.A. § 4005.
[4] *E.g., id.* § 4031(a).

the utmost good faith, honesty, and loyalty.[5] The violation of this fiduciary responsibility can lead to legal consequences.[6]

My wife and I have a sixteen-year-old son who is currently staying on a ranch with my cousin and his family in a neighboring state. He is helping work the ranch and attending school. To make things easy for my cousin and his wife, my wife and I prepared a general power of attorney granting them authority to act on our son's behalf. Having this document facilitated speaking to a school counselor, helping him get his driver's license, and signing field trip authorizations.

When does the power of attorney take effect, and how long does it last? There's some flexibility here, depending on the needs and wishes of the principal. It can become effective as soon as it's signed, which is often the case when someone needs immediate assistance with their affairs. The power of attorney my wife and I signed for our son took effect immediately.

Alternatively, it can be "springing," meaning it takes effect only when a specified event occurs, such as the incapacity of the principal.[7] A power of attorney in a trust generally takes this form. It may require, for example, a written determination by two physicians that the principal is mentally or physically incapacitated and unable to grant consent.[8]

The duration of the power granted can also vary. It may last indefinitely, end on a specific date, or terminate when a particular event occurs.[9] Depending on the jurisdiction, there may be a statutory limitation to its duration.[10]

A noteworthy variant of a general power of attorney is the durable power of attorney. The difference between a regular general power of attorney and a durable one is the latter remains in effect even if the principal becomes mentally incapacitated.[11] This feature can be critical in long-term planning, especially for seniors who may face declining health and want to ensure that someone can manage their affairs if they become unable to do so.

---

[5] *E.g., id.* § 4014.
[6] *E.g., id.* § 4017.
[7] *E.g., id.* § 4009.
[8] *E.g., id.* § 4009(b).
[9] *E.g., id.* § 4010.
[10] For example, in Idaho, the power of attorney for a minor cannot endure past six months generally, twelve months if the minor is serving abroad in the U.S. military, and three years if the power of attorney is granted to a grandparent, sibling, or aunt or uncle of the minor. I.C. 15-5-104.
[11] *E.g.,* 14 V.S.A. § 4004.

So you can set up a power of attorney that lasts until incapacitation (not durable), does not take effect until incapacitation (springing) or takes effect now and lasts through incapacitation (durable).

The authority to make medical or healthcare decisions for the principal often requires a separate healthcare power of attorney. Even though a general power of attorney can grant wide-ranging powers, healthcare decisions are usually considered too personal and sensitive to be included in a general mandate. We'll discuss those in the next section.

Although a general power of attorney grants extensive powers, there are some inherent limitations. An agent, for instance, generally cannot change the principal's will.[12]

Additionally, a general power of attorney can be revoked by the principal at any time, as long as they are mentally competent to do so.[13] Unless the power of attorney is durable, it will typically be revoked automatically if the principal becomes incapacitated and the agent becomes aware of the incapacitation.[14] It will also be nullified upon the principal's death,[15] at which point the executor named in the principal's will takes over the management of the estate.

Imagine one day you get in a skiing accident. You are airlifted to a hospital, where they induce a coma. For several weeks it is touch and go, and then once you're stable, you've still got a long road to recovery ahead of you.

What happens to your practice in that time? Your real estate holdings? The accident was traumatic enough. The last thing you want is to finally get your faculties back to discover that you've lost almost everything because you were the only one authorized to pay the bills, effectuate collections, and otherwise manage your financial affairs.

With a springing general power of attorney as part of your trust, you won't have to worry about that. You appoint someone you trust as power of attorney, and while you're incapacitated, they can take care of business. Literally.

A general power of attorney serves as a robust tool for managing a wide array of matters on behalf of the principal. From managing bank accounts and real estate to handling legal matters and more, the general power of attorney is an integral part of any revocable living trust. However, the broad powers granted by it bring along an equally

---

[12] *See, e.g.,* 755 Ill. Comp. Stat. Ann. 45/2-9.
[13] *E.g.,* 14 V.S.A. § 4010(a)(3);(b)(1).
[14] *E.g., id.* § 4010(a)(2); (e).
[15] *E.g., id.* § 4010(a)(1).

broad set of responsibilities and limitations that both the principal and agent must fully understand and respect.

Healthcare Power of Attorney

Whether the work you do in your particular medical field means you deal with the difficulties related to incapacitation, you can probably see the sense in anticipating this possibility. A healthcare power of attorney is a specialized legal document that grants a designated person the authority to make *healthcare* decisions on behalf of another individual when they are unable to do so themselves.[16] It is also known as an advance directive.[17] This authority is often necessary during emergencies, hospital stays, or instances of incapacitation where immediate decisions are required. Like the general power of attorney, the person who grants this authority is known as the principal, and the individual receiving the authority is termed the healthcare agent or attorney-in-fact.[18] Unlike a general power of attorney, which often encompasses a broad range of responsibilities including financial and legal matters, a healthcare power of attorney is limited strictly to medical and health-related decisions.[19]

Often, the requirement for activating the healthcare power of attorney is that the principal is no longer able to make decisions themselves, as certified by a medical professional.[20] This could be due to unconsciousness, severe illness, or mental incapacity. A healthcare power of attorney becomes invaluable in such situations, allowing the healthcare agent to act promptly, thus avoiding delays in treatment that could otherwise worsen the principal's condition.

The healthcare agent has the duty to act in the principal's best interest and must adhere to the medical preferences outlined by the principal in the document. These preferences can range from the kinds of treatment the principal is willing to undergo, to more intricate decisions about end-of-life care, including directives about resuscitation, ventilation, and feeding tubes[21] (discussed more in the next section). Additionally, the principal can include guidelines about

---

[16] ADVANCE DIRECTIVE, Black's Law Dictionary (11th ed. 2019).
[17] *Id.*
[18] *E.g.*, Cal. Prob. Code § 4701.
[19] *E.g., id.*
[20] *E.g.*, Md. Code Ann., Health-Gen. § 5-602(e)(1).
[21] *E.g., id.* § 5-602(d)(1).

pain management, organ donation, and even preferences for healthcare providers and facilities (also discussed in greater detail later in the chapter).

Ethically and legally, the healthcare agent is obliged to fulfill the principal's wishes as closely as possible, mirroring what the principal would have chosen if able to communicate. This fiduciary duty requires that the healthcare agent act with integrity, honesty, and in good faith. Failure to adhere to these principles can result in legal repercussions and even criminal liability in severe cases.

A healthcare power of attorney can work in conjunction with a living will, another legal document that outlines a person's wishes concerning medical treatment when they are unable to express informed consent. Although a living will specifies what measures should or should not be taken, it's the healthcare agent's responsibility to ensure that these wishes are carried out, acting as an advocate for the principal with the medical team and other family members.

Termination of a healthcare power of attorney happens automatically if the principal regains the ability to make decisions. Moreover, the principal has the right to revoke the document at any time as long as they are mentally competent. Any such revocation should be made known to all relevant parties, especially the healthcare provider and the appointed healthcare agent. The document also typically expires upon the death of the principal, unless there are specific clauses related to postmortem decisions like organ donation or autopsy.

With a focus solely on healthcare, this document complements a general power of attorney and is crucial for comprehensive life and estate planning. While it places a great deal of responsibility on the healthcare agent, it is a responsibility that comes with ethical and legal guidelines aimed at upholding the principal's wishes.

Life-Prolonging Measures

Although trauma-induced comas are relatively rare (approximately 258 adults out of 100,000 every year[22]), it doesn't

---

[22] Kondziella, D et al. "Curing Coma Campaign Collaborators: Incidence and Prevalence of Coma in the UK and the USA," 4(5) *Brain Communications* (2022), fcac188, available at https://doi.org/10.1093/braincomms/fcac188, last accessed September 11, 2023.

take much to have a plan if you are one of the unlucky few. Just a few paragraphs in your trust will do it.

For severe enough accidents that cause traumatic brain injuries, the mortality rate is somewhere between 76% and 89%, with those who do survive usually having a poor quality of life.[23]

In early 2010, my grandfather was in a car crash. He was found unconscious but alive. Paramedics rushed him to the hospital where he was plugged into several machines designed to keep him alive while the doctors tried to figure out what injuries he had suffered and what they could do to fix them.

They found significant brain injuries. They were confident they could keep him alive and unconscious with the help of machines but were equally confident that without the machines, he would either not survive or live in a vegetative (or near-vegetative) state with a very low quality of life.

He had a wife and seven adult children who loved him dearly. Because my grandpa planned ahead, he spared them the agony of having to decide together how to proceed. He had already made it clear that under this circumstance, he did not want his life prolonged by artificial means. The family honored his wishes and sent him lovingly to the other side.

A living trust is not complete without this important provision. Whether you wish your life to be artificially prolonged or not, you should make the decision now and potentially spare your family the heartache (and maybe infighting) of having to decide for you.

Organ Donation

If you're considering life-prolonging measures, it makes sense to think about organ donation at the same time. One organ donor can potentially save eight lives and enhance the lives of over seventy-five others.[24] Every ten minutes, someone else is added to the list, and at the time of writing, there were 104,234 people on the organ waitlist.[25]

---

[23] Steppacher I, Kaps M, Kissler J. "Against the Odds: A Case Study of Recovery from Coma After Devastating Prognosis," 3(1) *Ann Clin Transl Neurol. Dec* 61-65. (2015) doi: 10.1002/acn3.269.
[24] HRSA, "Organ Donor Statistics," available at https://www.organdonor.gov/learn/organ-donation-statistics, last accessed September 11, 2023.
[25] *Id.*

When you visit the DMV to get your driver's license, you are able to choose whether to opt in to organ donation.[26] You can also register at donatelifepa.org.[27]

Although if you are officially registered as an organ donor, your family cannot legally override your wishes,[28] in many cases grieving family members decline to donate their loved one's organs if there is no record of registration.[29] Moreover, even if the deceased is registered as an organ donor, most organ procurement organizations will honor the family's contrary wishes and decline to harvest the organs of donor whose families object.[30]

The inverse is also true. If you do not wish to be an organ donor, and therefore deliberately choose not to opt in (and therefore leave no record as to your wishes), your family can still choose to donate your organs.[31]

The best way to ensure your desires are honored—whether you want to be an organ donor or not—is to write them in a trust, have them notarized, and appoint a trusted trustee who has a fiduciary duty to make sure your wishes are upheld.

Guardianship Provisions – For the Testators

We've already discussed powers of attorney—documents that legally empower others to act on your behalf during temporary moments of incapacity—but what happens if you get to a point where such incapacity is long-term or permanent?

A guardianship is a legal mechanism by which a court designates a guardian—someone appointed to oversee the well-being and various

---

[26] *E.g.*, Arizona Department of Motor Vehicles, "Organ Donor Program," available at https://azdot.gov/mvd/services/driver-services/driver-license-information/organ-donor-program, last accessed September 11, 2023.
[27] https://donatelifepa.org.
[28] Unif. Anatomical Gift Act § 8(a) (amended 2006), 8A U.L.A. 76 (Supp. 2010).
[29] Strahilevitz, LJ. "The Right to Destroy," 114 (4) *Yale L.J.* 781, 854 (2005); List, J. "To Donate or Not: Is That the Question?" 7 (9) *Virtual Mentor*, 615–18 (2005). doi: 10.1001/virtualmentor.2005.7.9.msoc1-0509, last accessed September 12, 2023.
[30] Cotter, H. "Increasing Consent for Organ Donation: Mandated Choice, Individual Autonomy, and Informed Consent," 21 *Health Matrix* 599, 602 (2011).
[31] Spital, A. "Obtaining Consent for Organ Donation: What Are Our Options?", 13 *Ballière's Clinical Anesthesiology* 179, 181 (1999).

aspects of another person's life (called the "ward").[32] In some states, this is called a conservatorship.[33]

Although guardianships are most responsibly applied when an individual is no longer capable of making rational choices about their personal and financial matters or becomes vulnerable to manipulation or scams,[34] the reality is likely much less idealistic:

> Guardianship is a legal mechanism for substitute decision making which comes in the guise of benevolence, as it was originally intended to protect the disabled individual and his property from abuse, dissipation of resources, and the effects of designing persons. ... Yet, guardianship, in reality, reduces the disabled person to the status of a child. Few incompetent persons ever truly benefit from the guardianship system as practiced in ... most ... states.[35]

Britney Spears's case shone a light on the ugly nature of guardianship (called a conservatorship in California), which she was subject to for 14 years.[36]

Guardianships occur in less than half a percent of adults,[37] so there is a good chance it will never come to that for you. Even so, that number represents approximately 750,000 adults who have a guardian appointed.[38]

---

[32] *See* GUARDIANSHIP, Black's Law Dictionary (11th ed. 2019).
[33] California, for example. Cal. Prob. Code § 1800 et seq.
[34] National Guardianship Association. "What is Guardianship," (2019) available at https://www.guardianship.org/what-is-guardianship, last accessed September 12, 2023.
[35] *Matter of Guardianship of Hedin*, 528 N.W.2d 567, 572 (Iowa 1995) (quoting Sheryl Dicker, "Guardianship: Overcoming the Last Hurdle to Civil Rights For the Mentally Disabled," *U.Ark.L.Rev.L.J.* 485, 485–86 (1981)).
[36] Bowley, G. Nov. 12, 2021, *New York Times*, "Britney Spears Hearing: After Nearly 14 Years, Britney Spears's Conservatorship Ends," available at https://www.nytimes.com/live/2021/11/12/arts/britney-spears-hearing-conservatorship, last accessed September 13, 2023.
[37] Reynolds SL. "Guardianship Primavera: A First Look at Factors Associated with Having a Legal Guardian Using a Nationally Representative Sample of Community-Dwelling Adults," May;6(2) *Aging Ment Health*. 109–20 (2002). doi: 10.1080/13607860220126718.
[38] National Guardianship Association. "What is Guardianship," (2019) available at https://www.guardianship.org/what-is-guardianship, last accessed September 12, 2023.

The good news is, getting a guardianship requires proof that you're incapacitated in some way.[39]

In California, for example, this is allowed when there is sufficient proof to show either (1) that a person "is unable to provide properly for his or her personal needs for physical health, food, clothing, or shelter," or (2) "is substantially unable to manage his or her own financial resources or resist fraud or undue influence."[40]

In Britney's case, her father was able to prove that he should have the sole authority to manage her personal and financial affairs, stripping her of the ability to handle her own money (or even testify on her own behalf at court in an unrelated case[41]) based on evidence that she (1) shaved her head, (2) attacked paparazzi with an umbrella, and (3) locked herself and one of her children in a room to keep the child from their father.[42]

That's pretty alarming, if you think about it. She was demoted to the status of a child with evidence that was far from compelling.[43] With the publicity that came to this case when she ended the guardianship in 2022, hopefully future courts will be more circumspect about awarding involuntary guardianships.

Enter the trust. Although a trust can't guarantee a guardianship will never happen, having the powers of attorney will go a long way to preventing it:

> in most instances where an individual has, prior to becoming incapacitated, executed a health care proxy and durable power of attorney, the Court will not appoint a guardian, because the allegedly incapacitated person has effectuated a plan for the management of his affairs which obviated the need for a guardian.[44]

If you are truly incapacitated, and a guardianship is unavoidable, the trust will give voice to your wishes by allowing you to nominate two

---

[39] *E.g.*, 20 Pa. Stat. and Cons. Stat. Ann. § 5512.1.
[40] Cal. Prob. Code § 1801(b)–(c).
[41] *Lutfi v. Spears*, No. B246253, 2015 WL 1088127, at *4 (Cal. Ct. App. Mar. 11, 2015).
[42] Douds, GD. "Britney Spears's Conservatorship Case Explained," September 21, 2022, available at https://www.barrattorneys.com/blog/britney-spearss-conservatorship-case-explained, last accessed September 12, 2023.
[43] It's a good reminder that when there are as many different types of judges as there are personalities, there is no guarantee when it comes to the law.
[44] *In re Lowe*, 180 Misc. 2d 404, 405, 688 N.Y.S.2d 389, 390 (Sup. Ct. 1999) (internal quotations and citations omitted).

people (a first choice and a contingency) you wish the court to appoint as your guardian.

No one wants to have a guardian placed over them. With a properly drafted trust, we can manage your affairs in such a way that we hope a guardianship will be avoidable. If not, you'll at least have elected someone you have faith in to oversee your affairs while you are still alive but incapacitated.

Guardianship Provisions – For Minor Children

You have young kids.[45] If you (and their other parent) die while your kids are still young, who takes care of them?

You guessed it: it's whomever you appoint,[46] and if you don't appoint anyone, it'll be whomever the court appoints.[47]

It's difficult to say whom the court will appoint. It'll look to what is in the best interest of the child,[48] may take the child's own wishes into account if they're old enough,[49] and will likely first look to grandparents, aunts and uncles, or other family.

Instead of leaving your surviving family members to fight over who gets the kids (or who doesn't get them, as the case may be), and leaving the fate of your children to chance, best to nominate a guardian while you're still alive. And yes, this is another one of those important decisions that a good trust memorializes.

Best practices go beyond just nominating one person in your trust, though. Nominate at least two: your first choice and then an alternate (in case your first choice predeceases you, has become incapacitated themselves, or is no longer willing to take on the responsibility of raising your kids).

Speak to your nominees before signing the document. Make sure they understand what you're asking of them and are willing to do it.

---

[45] If you don't, feel free to skip to the next chapter.
[46] *E.g.*, Utah Unif. Prob. Code § 75-5-202.5. There are exceptions, of course. It's not always going to be the person you choose, especially if the other parent disagrees, the person you choose declines, or the court finds other good reason to choose someone else.
[47] *E.g., id.* § 75-5-206.
[48] *Id.* § 75-5-206(1)(a).
[49] *Id.* § 75-5-206(2); in Utah, they're old enough if they're at least 14.

As guardians, they'll effectively be your kids' new parents. They'll be responsible for their physical, emotional, social, spiritual, etc. well-being (i.e., all the things).[50]

You'll also want to make sure there are provisions in the trust that give your successor trustee (the one in charge of the assets in the trust after you die) authority to distribute funds from the trust to the guardians. These funds will pay for expenses related to your children and defray financial burdens the guardian incurs from raising and providing a home for your children.

Final Wishes or Funeral Instructions Document

The last of these important life questions we'll go over concerns your final arrangements. This includes how you want your remains to be disposed of, any final requests for your funeral, etc.

I recently attended my great-aunt's memorial service. She was the last surviving family member of her generation and had attended a lot of funerals in her final years. She insisted that at her service, there would be an all-you-can-eat taco bar catered by her favorite restaurant, Costa Vida (a growing chain of Baja-style Mexican food). It brought her family great pleasure to fulfill those wishes, and they repeatedly reminisced about her particular idiosyncrasy involving weekly taco outings.

At your funeral, do you want your brother-in-law to sing "Amazing Grace" accompanied by bagpipes? Or a karaoke version of Queen's "Another One Bites the Dust"? Do you have an uncle who shouldn't be granted any time with a microphone? Do you want to be buried at a specific cemetery? Cremated, with your ashes to be used to form jewelry or planted to become nutrients for a tree?

Now's your chance to make your wishes known.

Although your family will likely love having direction and be pleased to be able to grant you your final wishes, understand that these provisions of a trust are not necessarily binding.

Generally, there are no property rights in a corpse.[51] At most, there are quasi-property rights, though those belong to the family of the deceased, not to the deceased themselves.[52]

---

[50] *See id.* § 75-5-209.
[51] *See, e.g., Guth v. Freeland*, 96 Haw. 147, 154, 28 P.3d 982, 989 (2001).
[52] *Simpkins v. Lumbermens Mut. Cas. Co.*, 200 S.C. 228, 20 S.E.2d 733, 735 (1942).

Don't let that deter you, though. Just because it isn't legally binding doesn't mean your survivors won't move heaven and earth to make it happen. To ensure that your instructions are followed, may I offer the following advice:

1. Make sure you leave the instructions somewhere it will be sure to be found (keep a copy separate from your will/trust since those documents may not get pulled out until after your funeral).
2. Discuss your final wishes before death so whatever you have in your document won't come as a surprise.
3. Be kind to those around you. It will not only make it more likely they'll want to follow your instructions, but your life will be enhanced, too.

Also make sure whatever you request is legal. We had one client ask that his cat be buried alive with him. That's not just illegal; it's horrific. If it's legal and reasonable, go crazy! You only get one funeral.

CHAPTER 18

The Revocable Living Trust – A Seamless Transition of Property to Your Heirs

If you've ever heard a spiel on the importance of a living trust or read a blog article to that effect, it undoubtedly focused on avoiding probate.[1] And you probably had some idea of what probate meant, but perhaps didn't get a clear picture.

But now that you're this far in the book,[2] you realize that a trust does much more than just avoid probate. There is a whole world of benefits that occur while you're still alive.

Still, avoiding probate is pretty cool. So let me talk to you about that.

Probate is the process through which a court determines whether a will is valid.[3] It's also the process by which property is transferred when someone dies without a will.[4]

---

[1] *Off. of Disciplinary Couns. v. Yurich*, 1997-Ohio-239, 78 Ohio St. 3d 315, 319, 677 N.E.2d 1190, 1193 ("[E]veryone, regardless of their age, who owns real property, should consider a Living Trust for themselves. You may not realize it but your estate will eventually be controlled by your will, your attorney and the probate court, unless you consider a logical alternative. This alternative is a Living Trust.")
[2] Congrats, by the way. Thanks for sticking with me. We're in the home stretch now.
[3] PROBATE, Black's Law Dictionary (11th ed. 2019).
[4] *See, e.g.,* Wis. Stats. 852.

Put in simple terms: probate is litigation designed to transfer property that no longer belongs to anyone because its previous owner is deceased.[5]

To get a good idea of what that means, we need to turn to property law. Specifically, let's look at what it takes to transfer title to property while you are alive and then compare that with the process at death.

The law has a special term for the transfer of property during your lifetime. It's called an *"inter vivos* transfer."[6] *Inter vivos*, you can probably divine, is Latin for "between the living," or "while alive."[7]

An *inter vivos* transfer of property is very simple, but the mechanism for the transfer depends on the nature of the property.

In the case of a gift, transfer of ownership merely requires delivery of the property with intent that ownership transfers and acceptance by the person getting the gift.[8] This was a principle you learned early in life when you went to a friend's birthday party, handed them a package wrapped in paper, and then watched them open it. All your life, you have given and been given gifts, and every time, you were engaging in a legal, irrevocable, transfer of title.[9]

If you are exchanging property, like when you buy or sell something, the process is similar.

A transfer of real property, like land, is typically done via deed or even a writing approximating a deed.[10]

The transfer of a vehicle is usually as simple as signing its title.[11]

In some cases, specific statutory obligations must be met. For example, in Alabama, a manufactured home is considered personal property, not real property, so it is transferred using a certificate of title, not a deed.[12]

Regardless of the form of the property, the process is rather simple: either deliver the property with intent that it be conveyed or

---

[5] That's my definition. It may not be overly technical, but try to find one better that helps you understand what probate is.
[6] Do you still appreciate the Latin references? The law is replete with them, just like medicine is.
[7] *See* INTER VIVOS, Black's Law Dictionary (11th ed. 2019).
[8] *Rust v. Phillips*, 208 Va. 573, 578, 159 S.E.2d 628, 632 (1968); *Bader v. Digney*, 55 A.D.3d 1290, 1291, 864 N.Y.S.2d 606, 608 (2008).
[9] *Juliano v. Juliano*, 145 A.D.3d 983, 984, 44 N.Y.S.3d 482, 484 (2016).
[10] *Chebatoris v. Moyer*, 276 Neb. 733, 737, 757 N.W.2d 212, 216 (2008).
[11] 23 VSA § 2023.
[12] *Green Tree-AL LLC v. Dominion Res., L.L.C.*, 104 So. 3d 177, 184 (Ala. Civ. App. 2011) (citing Ala. Code § 32-20-30(a)).

deliver property with a signed document or writing evincing your intent that it be conveyed.

Billions of property transfers occur every day.[13] They're typically quick and easy.

But that's only true because you are alive.

Once you're dead, that's a different story. You can no longer deliver possession of the property. And you no longer have intent. What was simple the day before your death may have just become infinitely more complicated.

Now your heirs, those who believe they are entitled to your property, either because you've listed them in the will, or if you die without one, because they're closely enough related to you that the laws of your state will leave them something,[14] most likely have to go to court to get it.[15]

That means they'll likely have to hire an attorney, which means it will cost them. The attorney will open a court case, gather evidence, and present motions to the court, which in some cases will be disputed by other parties. There might be continuances, setbacks, and other delays. At some point, the court will make a decision, issue an order, and then the disputed property will be distributed according to the order, assuming neither party appeals the decision and continues the fight.

I had a case in probate court that illustrates just how ugly it can get. The deceased mother had a will leaving her roughly $3.5 million estate in equal thirds to each of her children. However, one of the children presented a false will to the court that named her as the sole beneficiary. For reasons I cannot explain (it predated my involvement in the case), the court acknowledged her will and granted her petition.

She took the money and ran.

In the meantime, we got the first order overturned with an order requiring her to return two-thirds of the property she had taken.

Not surprisingly, she wasn't very cooperative. At one point, the court ordered her arrested and kept in jail until she transferred the funds from an offshore account into an escrow account here in the U.S.

---

[13] I don't have a citation for this one, but as I picture every item purchased in every store by every person every day, I am confident I am right.

[14] Look up "intestate succession laws" in your state to get an idea of who would get what if you die without a will.

[15] There are exceptions. Different states have different rules, but if your estate is small enough, your heirs may not need to go to probate. *See, e.g.,* ORS 114.505 et seq.

She sat in jail for three months, refusing to give up on the ill-gotten stash of money, before the judge finally released her with the promise that she would turn in her passport within 24 hours. The judge wasn't willing to keep her in jail any longer, but intended to keep her in the country.

The woman did not turn over her passport. Instead, she fled the country, and, as far as I know, has never been heard from again.

I represented the public administrator in this case, so our involvement ended shortly after that, but I spoke to one of her siblings two years after my involvement ended. He was still spinning his wheels, doing everything he could to track down his share of the inheritance, the entire time spending good money going after bad and wishing for what might have been.

That's what probate court is. It's a fight over your money. And even if it's not a fight, it's not fun.

So what does a living trust have to do with this? The *living* trust, also called an *inter vivos* trust, is a living document (it's in the name) that constitutes a living entity, capable of owning things just like you and me.[16]

And that's where the magic happens—the trust lives and can own property. But that's not all. The trust has an enviable trait that, as human beings, we haven't quite been able to emulate: it cannot die.

A living trust will continue its existence past your death as long as you don't revoke it during your lifetime.[17]

It's that combination of simple facts that makes a trust so valuable after your death: it can own property and will outlive you. Add to that the fact that it will follow your directions, and you've got a winning combo.

Those directions are not limited to those we discussed in the last chapter relating to your lifetime. The trust is going to include within it a last will and testament that will identify your heirs and direct how your property is to be distributed among them.

Think about the implications of what we've learned about the living trust. If it is easy to transfer property belonging to the living, and quite a bit more difficult to transfer it if it belonged to someone deceased, then let's put our property in a trust so when we die, we

---

[16] *See, e.g., Nat'l Homeowners Ass'n v. City of Seattle*, 82 Wash. App. 640, 641, 919 P.2d 615, 616 (1996).

[17] *See* American Bar Association, "Revocable Trusts," available at https://www.americanbar.org/groups/real_property_trust_estate/resources/estate_planning/revocable_trusts, last accessed September 12, 2023.

don't actually own anything. The trust owns it all, and since the trust is still alive, it can make the transfer pretty easily. And it will do so according to the terms of the will within it.

But that means you have to transfer your property to the trust. And you're going to do that the same way you transfer any other property.

For your home, you're going to sign a deed transferring title to your trust (usually a simple-form deed like a quitclaim deed or warranty deed will do it); for your vehicles, you'll sign the title; and for your bank account, you'll go down to the bank to have them change it to the name of your trust.

For everything else: your laptop, your end table, your socks, etc., we're going to make it clear in the trust that you've conveyed it all to the trust (a pour-over will, which should be included in your trust, accomplishes that).

Remember, for a trust to be effective at avoiding probate, you must not only establish the trust but also transfer your property to it. Otherwise, your heirs could find themselves going to probate over the part of your estate you hadn't transferred to the trust.

Although not all estates are subject to the probate process (the smaller, simpler ones may not be, depending on your state), your choices in avoiding the process are typically going to be limited to (1) dying with few assets to speak of, or (2) creating and properly implementing a trust. Which one would you prefer?

There you have it! With your new understanding of living trusts, both their benefits during your life and those beyond, you should understand why the living trust is the central part of any estate plan.

CONCLUSION

In 2006, French marketing mastermind Clotaire Rapaille published a book called *The Culture Code*.[1] In it, he revealed a marketing strategy that he used to help international brands, like Honda, Boeing, Kellogg, GE, and L'Oreal, experience global success.

He conducted focus groups to discover the "code" or imprint of a product or brand: the innate emotions and unconscious meanings it evokes.

This approach revealed that struggling American manufacturer, Jeep, was going about their advertising all wrong. For Americans, it seemed, the Jeep was a metaphor for a horse—it represented expansion into an unexplored frontier. He recommended the auto manufacturer make their headlights round (horses have round eyes, after all). Jeep also pivoted in its advertising, leaning into the motif, and created commercials showing its vehicles racing through desert mountains, a trail of dust in their wake. Their sales increased dramatically.[2]

Similarly, for many Americans, the smell of coffee was imprinted on them at a young age as their parents held them close while sipping their morning cup. The lesson? Folgers should focus its commercials on the smell of coffee in the morning to reawaken those feelings of comfort and parental love. And you know what? You can probably still

---

[1] Rapaille, C. *The Culture Code*, 1st ed. New York: Broadway Books. (2006).
[2] That same messaging would not work in Europe, however. Europeans associated the Jeep with its introduction onto their shores at the end of World War II. Jeep's European code was "liberator." Jeep created a commercial with a Jeep that comes to the rescue of someone lost in the wilderness. And again, Jeep sales soared.

finish this line for me for one of the most successful commercial runs of our generation: "The Best Part of Wakin' Up ..."[3]

What does this have to do with you?

The "code" for "doctor," according to Rapaille, is *hero*.

That's how the American subconscious categorizes doctors. It also helps explain why when something goes wrong, and a patient doesn't get the outcome they want, you're to blame. You're the hero, but you didn't fix them.

That's a big archetype to live up to, especially if you're one of those human doctors.

I believe doctors are heroes, and I believe it is the actions, not the outcomes, that define heroes.

That's why I do what I do, and that's why I wrote this book.

In the preceding pages, we've covered what I call the four pillars of protection:

1. Protecting Your License
2. Protecting Your Assets
3. Protecting Your Income (Reducing Your Taxes)
4. Protecting Your Legacy

Like any other form of protection, there are no guarantees, except that if you don't use it, it won't protect you.

It is my hope that at least something in the book was beneficial to you, or if not that, then at least I made you laugh once or twice. Heck, I'd take a smile.

My goal is to do what I do so you can keep doing what you do.

---

[3] "... Is Folgers in Your Cup." But you already knew that.

FURTHER INFORMATION

If after reading this book, you realize you would like further information are looking for advice related to your circumstances and would like to speak to me or a member of my team, please feel free to reach out to us.

I run a law firm called the Fortune Law Firm. We are based in Las Vegas, Nevada, but do business with people nationwide. You can look us up at thefortunelawfirm.com and find out a little more about us there. You can also call us by dialing 725-245-1945 or email us at contactus@thefortunelawfirm.com.

If the person who answers the phone does not make your day better by at least putting a smile on your face, let me know. We take smiling very seriously around here.

ABOUT THE AUTHOR

Zach earned his law degree from the University of Illinois, graduating magna cum laude, and has since taught several university-level law courses and published over fifty legal articles, a legal-financial Amazon bestseller, *Unshackled: How to Escape the Chains of Conventional Wisdom that Keep You Poor*, and a criminal law book used as the text for a legal course at University of Nevada, Las Vegas.

For over a decade, Zach was a civil litigator and trial attorney who was able to win several multimillion-dollar judgments, expose the vulnerabilities of business entities, engage in veil piercing to destroy the corporate shield that litigants thought protected them, and find creative and diverse means to effectuate collection. As a first-chair trial attorney, he never lost. He lost twice as second chair, one of which was rectified on appeal. He is undefeated on appeal.

During his career as a trial attorney, he was no stranger to suing doctors. Medical negligence, it seemed, was everywhere. He took pleasure in holding medical professionals to account, though the more cases he resolved, the more he realized that the doctors were victims, too. Victims of a system built with doctors last in the line of legal priority.

In 2019, Zach sold his trial practice and shifted his focus. Now his time is spent helping doctors prevent lawsuits from ever happening, giving them as many tools to aid in their defense if it does, and keeping their assets protected should the case be resolved against them. To round out the protections, he provides estate planning, wealth creation, and strategies for tax reduction.

When he isn't wearing his lawyer hat, Zach spends his time in his garage workshop or traveling the world doing escape rooms with his wife and as many of their four kids as are available to join him.

ACKNOWLEDGMENTS

First, thank you to my wife of twenty years, Amber. She is as beautiful as ever (and probably more patient). Everything I do that's worth doing is possible with her unwavering support and encouragement.

I would not have the practical experience I do if not for the tireless efforts of my marketing partners at Fortress Management. Art McOmber and Joshua Johnson in particular, I am a better attorney because of all the medical professionals you introduce me to.

Huge thank you to my editor, Sarah Banks at Spring Tide Editing and Writing. I pride myself in my clear, concise, and typo-free writing, but Sarah proved over and over that no matter how many times I review the manuscript myself, there is always a benefit to having a competent editor seeing things the author cannot.

And of course to the many medical professionals who have had the trust in me to become my clients. It is your experiences and questions that became the basis for the topics covered in this book.

Made in the USA
Columbia, SC
03 November 2024